AURORA'S CURTAIN

Dare to Believe.

The End of the *Beyond Moondust Trilogy*.

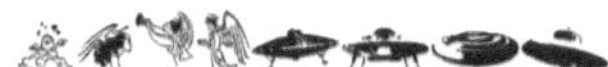

Volume 3

J.E. NICASSIO

"I prefer to speak of 'inter-dimensional' rather than 'extraterrestrials' because the latter has connotations of 'little green men' and all the other cliché responses. Nor does it tell the full story."

—David Icke

www.authorjenicassio.com

@jennie3963 www.facebook.com/jenicassio/

ISBN- 9780692994801
Published by NIEJE Productions LLC
Printed in the USA
Editor: Claudette Cruz
Proofreader: bzhercules.com
Cover Design: Dina Colangelo

1 THE NIGHTMARE BEGINS

I kept replaying what happened on the highway over and over in my mind. Two creatures soared in the sky above me, spraying flames over the highway like on a *Game of Thrones* episode. I remember diving in a ditch as the Thunderbird swerved, missing me but hitting fire at the black Escalade, engulfing it.

Lucien Foster and his brother, Cassiel, levitated in the air as balls of light shot from their hands in the bird's direction. I lay on the asphalt, watching in disbelief. I could see the bloody opening in my shirt.

The bullet must have gone straight through and out the other side. Funny thing—I wasn't in any pain—had to be the adrenaline pumping through my veins. But I saw everything happening to me like in a movie. A black sedan pulled up just when Lucien saw me.

"Sam!" he yelled.

I began to panic when I saw the men in military uniforms pull their weapons. He and Cassiel lowered to the ground, facing them unafraid.

Eden Foster arrived in the Jeep.

"Banth had to bring his pets. And I'm not in the mood to get my hands dirty today. Considering..." she said, peering at her manicure.

She began to fight the Thunderbird. More shots fired.

One of the Thunderbirds flew above me with its vast wings flapping inches from Lucien's head. "Lucien," I screamed. The prehistoric bird opened its mouth and sprayed flames at the ground. He stumbled and fell.

I cowered as the Thunderbird scooped Eden up. She glanced at me right before the beast hiked her up by the neck and dropped her flat on her stomach. She lifted herself up.

"That hurt!" she said. "You're making me angry now, big bird!"

For an instant, I saw huge flapping white wings in the wind.

I screamed as tiny wisps of feathers and ash fell on the ground around me.

The air was causing my lungs to tighten. The deafening sound of popping gunshots mixed with the sound of fire crackling made my ears ring.

"Lucien!" I yelled, keeping my face down toward the ground as I crawled to get to Lucien. "Eden, can you see them?" I yelled.

"I can't get to them." She kicked the Thunderbird as it dove near her. "I'm kind of busy at the moment!"

More black smoke. In a huge gust, the Escalade caught fire.

Eden lunged in my direction. "That was too close for comfort! Damn, that was close." She sprang to her feet and peered around.

Another Thunderbird fired. Cassiel stumbled and fell. I tried to see if Eden ran to him. "Sam! He's bad! Oh, no...I can't stop the bleeding!" she said.

Lucien was hit. The smoke filling my eyes stung, making it hard to see... "Cassiel!" He didn't answer.

A moment passed.

The smoke dissipated. Lucien and Cassiel lay on the highway. They weren't moving. Eden crawled to Lucien first and patted him down. "I can't tell where he's been shot!"

"Is he breathing... Eden, Lucien, are you, all right?"

She ran back to Cassiel.

I managed to crawl through the pain to Lucien and cradle his head in my arms. I propped up as much as I could to try and see Cassiel. He lay still.

Eden stood. She backed up and then she leaped into the air like nothing I'd ever seen. She was gone. Black boots approached me. Lucien opened his eyes and glowered with a sorrowful scowl.

I wiped the cinder and tears from my face.

"It's too late," Lucien said.

"No, no. I'll call for—"

My hands fumbled for my phone. I remembered

things more clearly than when it was happening. As if I were watching someone else's life.

* * *

2 GLORIA

Gloria gathered bloody gauze and surgical instruments from an alien that had gotten into a scuffle with one of Banth Radav's security units. She dropped what she was doing when two humans in scrubs wheeled in an injured human. Gloria watched Banth rush in behind the gurney.

"Out of the way, human!"

Banth's medical team prepped the human for surgery. "Get that corpse out of here!" Banth yelled.

Banth Radav, a tall, bald, human-like alien, stood at the foot of a surgical table.

"She's just about ready," the surgical technician said.

Banth leaned over and studied the new human's body. "Band her."

The technician took a plastic-like wristband and snapped it in place around the human's wrist.

Another tech took a small laser pen and a pad and tapped typewriting. He took the pen and scanned the band. Letters appeared on the band. The letters spelled out "Samantha Hunter."

"I trust you will do a good job."

He turned to the human abductee. "Gloria, I want you to tend to the wounds of this human when she comes out of surgery. Watch her every move."

Gloria nodded.

Banth stepped into Gloria's line of sight and grazed her cheek, pushing hair away from her face. "Do you understand?"

"Yes." Gloria flinched.

"I would hate to repeat myself, human."

"I understand."

"You best get clean bandages. You will need them."

Gloria obeyed Banth's orders. She left the operating room and hurried to the commissary. She passed rows and rows of human and alien DNA remains in storage. Embryos at different stages of development, located on the worst level of the compound — Perdition 7 dubbed the Pit. Gloria hated going there. She hated the vats with children's body parts. She always wondered who they had been. What were their names? Did they have a family at one time? She shifted around uncomfortably. Just the thought of being trapped on this level sent chills down her spine. It was the same level where Banth had tortured her. The military men were the worst when it came to pain. The cries, the beatings, the medical experiments... She wondered what Banth had in store for the human named Samantha Hunter.

Gloria hurried back to the medical lab where the new human was and stood in the background, watching.

"She has three gunshot wounds. If I don't operate soon, you will lose her," the doctor said.

"What're you waiting for? Get to it," Banth replied.

"Wait," Samantha Hunter said, barely audible. "What about the others?"

"Samantha, one of the bullets is close to a major organ. There isn't time to discuss the whereabouts of the Foster Clan."

3 SAMS ONLY HOPE

The pungent smell of antiseptic lingered in the cell, along with the same rotting odor of the No Whites from the fair. My arms and legs were strapped down. The cold metal table served as a cruel reminder that this was no nightmare; this was real life. Lucien and Michael must be dead, or close to it. I was barely alive when they threw me on the stretcher.

I went into space, was nearly killed at Area 51, and this is where I ended up? In a room with walls as gray as headstones? I coughed, feeling sharp pain radiate throughout my body.

Suddenly, a woman came in through the automatic door. I cringed as she walked toward me.

"It's ok. I'm not going to hurt you."

"You were helping Banth so why should I believe you?"

"I had no choice Samantha."

"How do you know my name?"

"You're banded."

Gloria's attention went to my wrist.

"This?" I tugged at the band that read Samantha

Hunter. Human DNA.

She nodded and went over to the basin to get water and dressings.

"Do you know why you're here?"

"Not exactly. Psycho Banth seems to think I'm some kind of a commodity because my blood mixed with Lucien's."

"This Lucien you speak of...is he human?"

"No."

She closed the distance between us. "Hold still. I have to change your bandages."

I watched her gently remove the tape from my skin. She began to unravel the gauze in a slow, almost poetic way. The wounds felt worse than they appeared.

"How many incisions do I have?"

"Three. What did you do to make Banth want to shoot you?"

"I don't think he meant to. But his cronies had other plans. I wish they'd killed me."

"You must be important."

"I wouldn't say that."

Gloria moved down to my side. "They just missed your spleen."

"How did I get here?"

"Most likely MJ12 foot soldiers."

"What's the fastest way out?"

"There is no escaping this place." Gloria became quiet.

"There has to be a way out. They got me in."

"You have no idea what this place is."

"Then enlighten me."

She walked over to the garbage can, threw away the bloody bandages, and grabbed some more gauze. She returned to my side, unraveling it, then lifted another bandage off my shoulder. "This one went clear through to the other side."

She was quiet a moment.

"I've been trying to leave this place since I was thirteen."

"How did you get here?"

"I was scuba diving with some friends in the Blue Hole. We went too deep. All I can remember is something grabbed my legs and pulled me into the cave. It wasn't human."

"The Blue Hole in Santa Rosa?"

She nodded.

"I've read stories about that. I thought they were urban legends. College kids were killed scuba diving, and days later, one showed up in Lake Michigan. You're one of them?"

"Yes."

"But you said you've been here since you were thirteen? You seem so young."

Gloria smiled.

My eyes searched hers. "How old are you?"

"I'm seventy-nine."

Aside from the splash of silver around her

hairline, her delicate features and lily-white skin showed no visible signs of aging. I noticed the notch in her chin, reminding me of Lucien. Don't go there. Any sanity I had left needed to be preserved in this underground hell.

4 LUCIEN

The October sun beamed on the steel roof of Foster Ranch. Lucien loaded a rifle magazine in the arsenal room. His hair had grown out since the firefight on the West Virginia Highway. Fleeting memories of his one true love consumed his thoughts. Why hadn't he run and taken Sam in his arms and told her how much he loved her? Why hadn't he altered time before Banth and his soldiers spilled her blood on the highway?

His brothers, Daniel and Gabriel, watched him without saying a word.

Lucien's sister, Eden, leaned against a counter. "Who do you plan on shooting?"

He turned his back to them, even though it wouldn't stop them from reading his mind.

He thought back to the highway once again. Samantha's anger was all he could see. And the sheer terror on her face when Banth appeared would be the only thing he'd remember if he didn't rescue her.

His anger grew as he socketed the magazine in place, set the AR down, and picked up another weapon. Cassiel had risked his life when he switched places with his brother on the ship. Then he'd given his life for Samantha.

Michael lifted his hand, and a virtual computer screen appeared—a giant Google map of the state. Jordan Foster picked up a weapon and started to load it alongside Lucien.

Lucien could feel the tension, but he kept his focus on Samantha.

"You're not really going to let him search for her, Uncle? Tell me you're not."

Eden's tone caught Lucien's attention, but all he could think of was killing Banth and saving Samantha. She was somewhere hurt and alone—or worse.

Jordan may have been frail from the heart attack he'd suffered, but he still oversaw the Fosters. Lucien knew Jordan was the glue that held them together and respected him for that.

"Uncle? Are you?" Eden asked.

Jordan continued loading his weapon. "I haven't decided."

"You shouldn't be stressing about this mess. You're still weak. Don't let him pull you into his drama."

"Eden, if you ask me, you're the one causing the stress," Michael said.

"What are you searching for?" she snapped.

"The geography of the area he may have taken

her to."

Lucien glanced up at the screen.

"Why even bother with Google maps? It's impossible to figure out where they took her."

"Her! Her! Her name is Samantha!" Lucien bellowed.

They stopped what they were doing and looked at Lucien.

Gabe chuckled, but when no one else laughed, he shifted his position and cleared his throat.

Lucien turned his back to them again, not saying another word, and continued loading more bullets in a high-powered rifle. His thoughts once again went to Samantha, ricocheting in all directions as he replayed the firefight in detail, leading up to when he collapsed on the highway. He tried to think back... Did he recognize any of the men in boots on the freeway?

He wiped away a new coat of sweat that had beaded up on his brow. A drop landed in his eyes, stinging and blurring his vision, which caused him to let go of a bullet.

Jordan bent down to pick it up. Lucien intercepted before Jordan's slight frame bent forward. "It's been days since you had any sleep, son. Stop this and go get some rest," Jordan said.

"When you were brought back to the ranch, you were almost dead. Tell him, Uncle!" Eden said.

Jordan didn't answer.

"Our uncle had Division Six bring surgeons to operate on you. When they were working on you, Jordan had another heart attack. That one was serious, but luckily, the medical team was still here," Gabe said.

Lucien glanced at Eden a moment and saw the pain in her eyes.

"Son, put the weapon down. You need to rest," Jordan said.

Lucien took a breath and sighed. His uncle was right, exhaustion was going to be his rival. Pain still tore through him from the gunshots he'd received on the highway.

He ignored his uncle.

"We know that Banth has her and maybe Project Blue Book's agents are involved, by the guise of the men in uniform," Michael said.

"Banth is working with the government? That's insane," Eden said.

"We haven't heard anything about Landson Shaw or Nathan Moore. It was like they disappeared."

"They haven't. I think the two are sitting low for the time being. It's a wait-and-see game right now," Jordan said.

"Sam's father keeps calling and wanting to talk with his daughter. We are running out of excuses to tell him."

"What are we supposed to say when he calls

again, Brother?"

An uncomfortable moment passed. A chill crept down Lucien's shoulders. He took a bullet in his fingertips. His hand trembled, making it difficult for him to continue to load his weapon. He paused, giving Eden an invitation to speak.

"Do we even know where they took her?" Her firm tone echoed throughout the armory. No one answered. Each of the siblings looked over at the other with a blank expression.

"Come on! We lost Cassiel. I don't want to lose anyone else is all I'm saying." She charged in Lucien's direction.

Michael put out his arm to stop her.

She gave him a sharp glare.

"Look at me! We could get in touch with Dejaha Zoris. He'll help us since he was tricked by Banth as well!" Eden yelled so loudly, the tiny veins that ran down her neck looked twice their size.

"I wouldn't count on him assisting us," Jordan said.

"Then what, Uncle?" Daniel said. "Brother, are you even listening?" Daniel approached Lucien as he continued to load the weapons.

"It's no use, Daniel, he's consumed with anger and hate right now. It's best we leave him to his thoughts," Jordan said.

Daniel shrugged and left the room.

Michael swiped the invisible computer screen,

making it disappear. "You better snap out of it!" he said.

Eden looked back at Lucien one last time before she left the armory, following her brother's cue. The room was quiet except for the bullets being loaded.

Jordan put the weapon he was loading on the countertop and watched them leave. He stood near his nephew. "Lucien..."

He didn't answer.

"Lucien?" he shouted.

Lucien still ignored his uncle.

Jordan took hold of the weapon in his hand and held it tight within his grip. "I may be old and decrepit, but you're still no match for me."

Lucien let Jordan think he had the upper hand when all he had to do was think and the weapon would go slamming into the wall with just a thought.

Jordan's leathery, sun-bleached hand steadied upon the weapon as he spoke.

His nephew stopped and released the weapon in his hand. And listened to the only father he'd ever known.

"You can load every weapon here with the intent of killing Banth and Project Blue Book's men and every mutant, but this silence is not going to find Samantha Hunter."

"You'd have me do what, then? Sit here and lick my wounds like an injured animal?"

"If need be, or until your injuries have healed.

Your wounds go deeper than the physical scars, my boy. It will give your brothers time to locate Miss Hunter's whereabouts."

Jordan put the weapon on the counter and slowly turned his aged body to leave.

"I didn't raise you to want to kill like the others. I raised you to be better than that. You are better than that. You hear me, Luci—"

"They murdered Cassiel."

"I'm well aware."

"You say that like it's nothing." Rage tore through him like a riptide on a full moon.

"You are acting worse than Cassiel did last Halloween."

"There is no comparison!"

"How so? Your rage is like a snake's poison eating into your flesh."

"Cassiel only cared about leaving Sam to die. He didn't want me to save her. But he did not deserve to die at the hands of Banth!"

"Your brother was lucky he lived as long as he did. Anger consumed him; it almost cost you your life. That night on Halloween, he could have killed you, as I recall."

"He didn't deserve to die." He studied Jordan's reaction as light glistened from his gray eyes.

"No one deserves to die, son."

"Banth does."

"You are not his judge."

"Who is...God. Your God?"

Jordan smiled. "Your father's and mine."

"I have no father; they had him murdered in nineteen forty-seven."

"Lucien...."

"Banth took Sam, and he killed my brother."

"And he will be found and punished."

"What am I supposed to do until then?"

"Think and solve the issue."

"He's a murderer. They killed Cassiel in cold blood. One of their own kind."

"Yes, it's a damn shame he was killed. He made a choice to be there. When you were called back to your family's ship, he took your place. He felt it was his duty to protect Samantha because of his love for you. We all must live with the choices we make."

"Then I must avenge him and punish Banth."

"You're going at it in the wrong way, my boy."

"I have to find her.

"And you will."

5 BLOOD

It seems like months since I've been brought here. Here must be must be Dulce, New Mexico. The underground compound that Michael and Cassiel told me about on the drive back from Area 51.
"Let me out of here!"

The light flickered on as I pounded on the metal door. I began to pace and yell. The room was no bigger than my old bedroom in Pittsburgh.
"You can't keep me here. You hear me, alien?"

"You're wasting your breath, human," the guard said.

"Let me out, you bastards!" I couldn't see him, but I could smell him. A cross between road kill and urine.

I thought back to what Gloria had said. MJ12 foot soldiers and Banth brought me here. She told me he was working with the government. But for how long? Gloria herself was a captive not allowed to leave Dulce. They were keeping her here for God knows what reason. She spent her entire adult life stuck in this hellhole of a nightmare just like me.

I inspected the area of my gray cell. My new

home! This was my punishment for loving a supernatural being. But Lucien wasn't like anyone here. He appeared almost human, not like these gross, disgusting creatures. This was Dante's Inferno. I could hear the alien behind the metal door, daily through the intercom taunting me, humiliating me. It would wake me up every hour on the hour just for kicks and giggles. He wasn't human for sure, and he let meknow it. Gloria told me all those stories about alien abductions were hoaxes. There were no space crafts from outer space, and this was something the government fabricated long ago. Why would the government make this all up? What was in it for them?

I pounded on the metal door again and again and again until my hands were bleeding and raw. My feet padded on the cold cement floor until they were red and too blistered to walk. I faltered back to the door and rested my ear against its smooth, chilled surface, hoping and praying it would open and be Lucien. I was just about to put my fist on the door again when it opened. In walked Banth and another man.

"Samantha, this is Raul Roman," Banth said.

The man wearing a white lab coat approached me.

"He's going to take a blood sample. We really do need to clean you up a bit though, and this...piss pool. You have to be at your healthiest."

Raul approached, taking my arm. I pulled away.

"Don't touch me!"

He retook my arm and lifted it over my head.

"What are you doing?"

Then he took my other arm.

"Stop it!"

"Samantha, we need to find a good vein."

I backed away. "You can't be serious. I'm not letting Dr. Frankenstein near me."

"He's the finest genetic engineer your Earth has to offer. You're in good hands. I promise," Banth said.

"What do you need a genetic engineer for?"

"He has work to do. Again, I promise you—"

"Like your promise means anything to me."

Banth's grayish complexion and shiny bald head still gave me the creeps more than the "No Whites" at the fair. But it was his beady olive eyes haunting and taunting me every night with nightmares I disliked the most.

"Now, now, Samantha, sticks and stone may break my bones." He read my mind. "What is the rest of the rhyme?"

"But words will never hurt me," I said, humoring him.

"Isn't that one of your childhood rhymes here on Earth?" He laughed, showing his jagged teeth.

I cringed once more.

"What did you mean by good vein!" I backed

away into the corner.

Raul Roman took a syringe from his pocket.

"Stay away from me! You don't have the right to do this!"

The metal door opened with two military guards coming straight for me. One on each arm. My legs went kicking.

"We just need a little blood to make sure conditions for the procedure are viable," Raul Roman said.

"What procedure? You're both insane!"

"Maybe just a tad." Raul Roman held the long needle in my direction. *There's no place like home, there's no place like home.* Raul Roman's expression clearly said he enjoyed torturing me.

"No! Don't come near me. You monster!"

I spat at him.

He wiped his face and then wiped his hand on his lab coat.

"Samantha, I would be kind to the man who's going to take blood from you. You know they have bigger needles to do the job here. Do you want me to go fetch one!" Banth said with a smirk.

"No." I took a breath, feeling defeated. Raul Roman came close.

I backed away again.

He gave me a sickening smile and kept getting closer.

My foot had a mind of its own, and I kicked him in the nut sack.

He bent forward, yelling, "You little bitch!"

I started to laugh—not the best idea.

The guards released me; I guess they were worried they were next.

My breath caught the nagging pain where they had stitched me off guard.

"You are a spunky one, I have to say, Samantha!" Banth laughed.

"Not for long!" Raul Roman spat back.

"Nonsense! Hold that needle steady."

I held the side where one of Banth's men shot me on the highway. The more I got upset, the more I hurt. I should just keep my mouth shut and let them torture me some more.

The guards retook my arms and threw me on the cot.

"Send in two more guards," Banth spoke into his wrist phone.

Two guards came rushing in through the metal doors. My arms and legs thrashed out like I was a wild animal fighting for its life before it got skinned. They took my legs and held me down.

Raul Roman grinned, took a band, and tied it tight. He poked my vein with the needle. An electric shock shot clear up to my shoulder.

"I hit a nerve," Raul Roman said, smiling.

Banth gawked, also smiling.

"Good."

I cringed and watched the blood fill the plastic

container. I struggled, but they were too strong for me. Raul Roman released the needle and eyeballed me straight in the eye.

"I hope it hurt."

I ignored him and turned my head before he saw a tear escape. "How long are you going to keep me here?"

He didn't answer.

Banth rubbed his temple.

The guards released me.

"I have no intention of ever letting you leave, Samantha. I thought you'd figured that out by now. You're too precious," said Banth.

"Precious?" I wanted to scream.

His translucent skin quivered and his bald skull pulsated with visible veins that throbbed.

"I've become quite attached to you. Besides, you're priceless, my dear. And time is running out. We have to move quickly."

"For what? What're you planning—to take over the world?" I started to laugh, but I wanted to cry instead.

"You have no idea what's developing, but soon you will."

I rubbed my arm where the needle pierced me. "You're a sick bastard, you know that!"

"I've been called worse, my dear. But for some reason, coming from you, it makes me all fuzzy inside."

"You make me sick."

He rolled his thin lip and nodded his head like he thought it was a compliment. His foul mouth opened as if to speak, but he said nothing.

"What? Tell me!" I sat up on the cot. "Tell me!"

He only smiled.

"I hope the Fosters find you and kill you!"

Banth chuckled. "The Fosters? They are well enough, but, how do you say, out of commission for a while."

"What did you do! You left them there to die, didn't you? You're sick, sick, sick."

"Yes, maybe, but not as sick as humanity right now."

"You killed them?"

"The Fosters and about ten million earthlings."

I felt tears beginning to well.

"The virus?"

"An unfortunate event."

Raul Roman and his guards turned and left my cell. I watched the sliding door open and close. Its heavy metal made a swooshing sound that echoed through my little entrapment. I just sat there ogling at it to magically open so I could run.

"Where would you go? After the boy? Hmmm," Banth said, observing me, reading my mind. "You tickle my curiosity, my dear. You... What do they call it? Love the Foster boy."

I didn't answer.

"I don't quite understand this human emotion. It intrigues me. I would like to learn more."

"You're not learning from me."

He folded his arms, not saying anything more.

"Are you just going to stare at me for your enjoyment?" I sighed, still rubbing where Raul Roman had poked me with the needle.

Defeated, I rolled over on the cot, not caring if Banth was still there. I sat up when I heard the doors open. Gloria brushed shoulders with Banth when he went out the door. They made eye contact but did not say anything. The grimace of disgust on Gloria's face clearly communicated her feelings for Banth.

The door closed behind Banth.

"Are you, all right?" She sat down next to me. "I saw Raul Roman and his guards." She grimaced. "What were they doing here?"

"They took blood from me."

"They hurt you?"

"Well, yeah. Do you know anything about it?"

"I would tell you if I did."

I raised an eyebrow and sat up. "Really?" "I would. Why would I keep anything from you?"

"Because you seem to be Banth's pet."

"No. I despise Banth more than you'll ever know."

I sprang from my cot and began to search every nook and crevice of my cell. I patted the walls for something, anything, to get me out of here.

"What're you doing?" Gloria said, following me.

"What does it look like? I'm trying to find a way out of this hellhole!"

"Samantha, there's no way out. I thought I made that clear."

"There's got to be. Banth has to get supplies in here some way."

"Supplies are brought every ninety days."

"How do you know day from night? There are no windows."

"The alarm rings and the guards announce it."

I glanced at her skin. A face without sunlight would never age like people above.

"Guess you don't need to worry about sun spots, huh? Just think of all the anti-aging cream you don't need to fuss with. That's a plus to living underground."

I stopped and studied her facial expression for some clue of what she was thinking. "I want to get sun spots on my skin and use old-age cream. I'm getting out of here if it's the last thing I do."

"There isn't a way out. You're Banth's prisoner and the Ultras', Maji."

"Who are they?"

"Banth's alien government."

"A government of whom? Project book and MJ12?"

"The different races of alien. They work

together."

"His minions?"

"I don't understand."

"Who do his evil doings."

"Yes."

"What do they want?"

She just stood there with a stupid expression on her face, not answering me.

"Gloria, you're making this really... Never mind. Just tell me."

"There's no way out. I already told you, if there were, I would have been long gone. They want you," she whispered.

"Gloria...that's obvious. But why?"

* * *

I thought back to that day at the Fosters' ranch. With Jordan Foster, Cassiel, Michael, Daniel, Eden Nathan Moore, and Agent Harmon and thirteen-year-old Dusty Kats. Having dinner around the formal dining room table. I remembered what Jordan told me about Dulce.

* * *

The Grays are trying to create a superior race, using their DNA and tweaking it a little at a time with cross-breeding. A little of this and a little of that, to make it sound simple.

* * *

This couldn't be what they were referring to.

I snapped back to the present.

"He wants my DNA?"

"Banth wants what he cannot have. To be human," Gloria said.

"He and the 'No Whites' have been trying to get their paws on me all year? They want my DNA to help them create some sick race. That has to be it."

"Samantha, you are correct and—"

"What aren't you telling me!"

"You've come to a devious place."

"I kind of figured that one out. I have to get out of here."

I gave Gloria a quick, curious expression. "Did you really try to escape this place."

"Years ago, when there was a firefight."

Gloria turned her back.

I grabbed her shoulder to face me.

"I don't like thinking about it."

"You have to. Snap out of it. There may be a clue to help me find a way out."

"Many died that day! Too many."

"No! Some made it. There's a place called Greenbrier. I've been there. There are hundreds, young and old hybrids. And humans helping them survive. It used to be a safe house for the United States Senate. Now it's a mock resort in West Virginia. But, behind the walls, it's a secret bunker. During the Cold War years ago, it was used for the United States Senate and the president to reconvene if there was a nuclear war. That's where we were coming from when Banth and his buddies attacked us. I've seen it with my own eyes, Gloria. They made it."

"That's not true."

"I tell you it's true. It's in Greenbrier, West Virginia."

"How do you know this?"

"There was a young hybrid named Dusty Kats that needed refuge. I went along with the Fosters to take him there."

"You are important, then, if you were involved with them and they took you to this place, Greenbrier."

"I didn't have a choice."

"You were being protected, so you are important."

"Banth wanted me... I know that. But I will kill myself before I let him use me."

"Experiments?"

"That's not going to happen to me!"

"That's why Banth took you."

"Why Dulce?"

"Dulce wants something from all of us."

"And I'm not about to give it to them."

"You have resolve and courage. I don't anymore. That was taken from me. I'm too old and tired."

"Gloria, you have to help me."

"What can an old woman possibly do to help

you leave this place?"

I peered around the cell again. A moment passed before I walked up to the motion detector and moved a chair and stood on it.

"What are you doing?"

"There has to be something here."

A small, round device fitted over it. I fiddled with it, hoping I could figure out how to turn it off. "It's a magnet." I moved it again, jiggling it back and forth, trying to loosen it.

I removed the plate while Gloria watched on.

"This is so small. What could it possibly be for?"

"It's a sensor."

"To what?"

"A heat sensor."

"To measure body heat? Well, whatever it did, it's not going to be working anymore." I turned it around. "It's a magnet."

"The aliens call them 'Lodestones,' a naturally magnetized mineral."

"What're they doing with magnets?"

"It's their energy source."

"It seems so primitive."

"Banth intends to continue to harvest the power and use it to destroy humanity."

"So, they think."

"The aliens use Magnetite' power in everything."

"Magnetite power?"

I stopped to listen to her.

"They have been harvesting lodestones for centuries. They hope to consume all the Magnetite power of the Earth."

"It makes sense now. Like in cell phones, MRIs, computers? You have no idea what I'm talking about to you? Oh course, you wouldn't being underground so long."

"The aliens showed the government how to use magnetic power. They gave their alien technology as a bargaining tool to the government in exchange to experiment on humans and study them. The magnetics keep us enslaved."

"It's the devil's work..." I turned the knob. "Augh. Ugh. Come on, Sam. You're turning to mush here."

Out popped a greenish glow. "Christ!"

Basketball-sized orbs came out and fluttered around the room. I almost fell when one swooped down, almost smacking me in the head. I hunched over, trying to avoid being hit. Gloria mimicked me.

"What are these!"

The silent orbs flew quickly around the cell. They began to hum. "They are unmanned patrol drones."

"Drones!" I ducked again, trying to avoid being hit once more.

Gloria bent when one almost hit her. "The humming sound is it taking pictures of humans. The glow is a magnetic aura. The green light is a visible spectrum of magnetic power, but the light does not reflect."

"I had no idea they could do so much!"

"Magnets are everywhere here. Copper too...one of its primary uses is to contain the magnetic flow. Everything at Dulce is lined with copper."

"What do they use the copper for?" I asked.

"The copper blocks the hybrids from using their powers."

"So, the hybrids become their bitches."

"That may be what the sensor is for," Gloria said.

"Not anymore."

Gloria gave me a puzzled expression. "The exterior walls are steel," Gloria said.

"I guess nothing is getting past that, then."

The orbs swooped down and opened the metal door of the cell. I shrugged in disbelief. The doors shut fast.

"Little spies."

"They're much more than that."

"Well, between you and me, I really don't want to find out what else they do."

"Where does Banth stay?"

"On Level Four."

"Level Four?"

"Yes, there are several cells there."

Just like Michael and Cassiel said there were.

Gloria's demeanor changed. She paused, struggling to speak.

"Are you, all right?" I moved closer to her.

"The cells on the fourth level are made of lead, then a massive magnetic steel that's covered in copper." She stopped and took a breath. "They contain the essence of what you would call a disembodied living soul."

I cringed.

"They take the souls from humans."

"That's insane! They can't do that to people."

"But they do!"

"Is Banth behind this?"

"He and the others."

"Others? You mean like aliens?"

"Yes." Gloria paused, almost coughing out the words.

"Who are these other aliens?"

"Alternative 3, it's an elite military service. The joint alien-Illuminati."

"Harmon's soldiers." I thought back to the underground massacre at Greenbrier. "But he wanted to kill the hybrids."

"And your government."

"Human beings are allowing this to happen? Is this true? You're telling me the government is truly behind this?"

"And a few other nations."

"The UN is involved?"

"I don't know specifically if the United Nations as a whole."

The Fosters weren't exaggerating. It was real, everything and everyone was speaking the truth. I must find a way out of here. Michael said there are seven levels. And a central core. But where is the main level to get out of here?

My heart began to pump hard in my chest, and my hands took Gloria by the shoulders and shook her. I didn't stop until the grimace on her face turned to fear.

"Gloria, you have to tell me what is on the other levels. Where is the central core?" She just stood there dumbfounded. Like I was crazy. I guess I was at this point.

"Answer me! Gloria, don't freeze up. I need you to stay focused." She didn't answer. "Is the whole complex wired with cameras?"

She just stood there with a blank expression.

"Answer me!"

Gloria walked over to the cot and sat down. "Yes...but you mustn't think these things, Samantha. They can read our minds."

"Oh, of course, they can!" That was one thing I hated about Lucien. My thoughts were never my own. I sat down next to her. "Okay...what else?"

"They have scanners that measure body heat."

"How do they work?"

"Not sure, they just do."

"What else?"

"What does it matter?"

"Because I am not staying here until I am seventy-nine living in this hell. That's why."

"You're wasting your time."

"Gloria...I am not staying here."

"You can't leave this place. If there was a way out, don't you think I would have escaped?"

"Okay...okay, okay. The aliens live on sub-levels. Damn, I can't remember. I wished I'd paid attention to Cassiel and Michael. They said there were safe houses. Where are the safe houses? Who lives in them? Gloria, who?"

"There are too many to mention."

"Where do the Gray Skins live?"

"The Grays are not the worst. The lizard people, Banth calls them the 'Removers.'"

"What do they remove?"

"The humans that bore him."

"I wish I didn't ask."

"They are the Reptoids—the devil's favorite."

"You mean Banth?"

"There are many different races here. They are all devious."

I began to pace the cell. "What else?" I ran my hands through my tangled hair.

"There are a few who are not. And they are the hybrids. And there are the abductees."

"Have they given up like you?"

She grimaced. "They've formed a Resistance." Her voice became a whisper. Gloria motioned me to sit with her. She kept her voice at a whisper. "They can hear everything we say."

"Tell me about this Resistance."

"A group of hybrids, humans."

"Is it Division Six? No." I answered my own question. "They're protecting the hybrids, it wouldn't be them. Or could it be them?"

"Samantha, there's something you should know. They plan to take over Banth soon."

"Like years ago," I remembered Michael saying this. "But only twenty or so escaped."

"Yes, like before, but they are confident they will succeed this time."

"When?"

"There's a meeting in a safe house on Level Three, just after midnight."

"You're taking me?"

"The others will not be happy. They may think you're Banth's spy."

"I'm going."

A moment passed.

"I will be back to get you."

Gloria's expression changed. A painful scowl on her face appeared. She grabbed her arm and grimaced. A tattoo-like marking began glowing red.

"What's this?" I said, taking hold of her wrist.

"Banth is summoning me. He implanted a communication device in my arm. When it glows, it causes an electric shock."

"That's barbaric!" I released her arm.

"I will return after I do Banth's bidding."

I watched her leave, wanting to go through the sliding, swishing doors with her.

6 CELL 3

Gloria's hands shook as she pulled on a pair of latex gloves. She bent down on her hands and knees and began to scrub the floor in Cell B. The blood just seemed to pool and not go anywhere on the tile floor as she made circular motions. She squeezed out the bloody water from the sponge. The metallic smell made her stomach queasy. This was an average day for her being Banth's slave. She was thankful for the gloves she traded for. She bargained a hybrid for a cube of sugar to get them.

Gloria mused on Tarragon's meeting with the Resistance's group of hybrids and abducted humans— Older, Noah, Rek, and a dozen more. While she pondered, she took a mop and splashed it in the pool of blood, hoping it would work better to clean the area. When the mop hit the floor, blood sprayed on her cheek. Gloria wiped it fast. She thought about the stories of how people had never returned from Cell B.

She hurried and put the mop away and grabbed the trash bag. Tick tock, tick tock was the only sound, from the clock on the wall. Gloria glanced at it briefly and began to hurry.

The lights automatically shut off when she stepped out the door. She paused and took a deep breath before she set out down the tunnel. She winced through the mutedly lit rock underpass where the Gray-skinned slept.

Gloria trudged the tunnel's ominous narrow shaft when an alien with giant tentacles and limbs bounded at her. The alien resembled a human except its skin was as pale as snow and its forehead twice the size as most humans, with gold-colored eyes. The alien's hands worked on an electronic equipment in the cavern.

He glared at Gloria.

She tried to avoid eye contact by lowering her head as she passed the Orieni base's domain. Banth told her they possessed a power to hypnotize their victims and lure them back to their lair. What they did to their victims was a mystery because no one survived to talk about it. Gloria moved fast here, gazing at the passageway enclosed by security and arsenal.

The Orienis maintain the tunnels, she thought. They're in constant battle with the Reptilians and the Gray ones.

Gloria knew anyone that entered Level Five had high clearance. And she had it. She got her clearance from Banth. For some reason, Gloria felt Banth trusted her. Little did he know she despised him.

Every time Gloria went to Level Five, she had to be accompanied by the special military unit called Ultra Seven.

She came upon an alien guard.

"Where is your escort, human?"

"Ugh ...none were available."

"The alien housing is off limits to any hybrid or human unless they have permission. The tunnel is enclosed by advanced security, and we are trained to kill at will. And some get mighty bored down here."

"I have clearance. These need to be incinerated." She lifted the garbage bag.

Gloria held out her arm, showing the implant that was engraved on her like a branding ranches did to their cattle.

The guard peered at the tattoo of triple Xs that was Banth's clearance code. The alien military foot soldier pointed a weapon at Gloria.

"I said I have clearance." Gloria raised her arm again in the direction of the alien guard, showing no fear.

"Make it quick, human!"

She paused a moment. The guard pushed the weapon into her side. "Come on, human, you're taking too long. I could shoot you and feed you to the Orienis." He nudged Gloria with the weapon.

She kept her head down while her hands fumbled with the trash bag, dropping its contents everywhere. "Looks like you don't care for this level?"

The alien observed her. "You clumsy human. A good human is a dead human, what I always say."

Gloria hurried.

"Could you be any slower?"

Gloria grabbed the dropped bandages and blood-stained clothing. She ignored the guard and took the trash bag and hurriedly put the garbage in and tied it quickly.

She turned to the guard. "Okay. I'm done."

They jaunted through a trailer-sized tunnel strung with lights from the ceiling. Gloria made haste, pausing a few times to scan a green phosphorescent glow. The guard nudged her shoulder when they approached a crossroad area.

"Hurry," the guard said.

The tunnel merged with the sewer system and led to the Blue Hole where Gloria herself was taken.

She mused in wonder how the United States' government could allow such an evil place to exist.

The guard shoved Gloria onto a horrid maze-like passageway. She stumbled at the entrance to one of the cells. When she did, a jade-colored light shone upon them.

Gloria halted as if her feet were superglued to the ground. She stood firm in her bare feet, paralyzed.

Her chin dropped, and terror catapulted through her like an electrical shock. She gazed up slowly at a seven-foot Reptilian humanoid named Snake. The creature peered at her. Goop dripped from his mouth. His yolk-colored eyes glowed in the dim lighting. He scraped off nonexistent dirt between his claws and studied her.

"A few of us agree that you are among the missing. It has begun," replied Snake.

"What does that mean?" she whispered, afraid to raise her voice. The guard froze, staring with terror radiating from his eyes.

Gloria instinctually pushed the guard's arm, breaking the trance. She seemed unscathed as if it were a regular occurrence.

"You know better than to stare them directly in the eyes," she said to the guard.

Speechless, the two of them hurried through a vast hall leading to the upper levels. Gloria rallied past Snake as he yelled, "You are among the missing!"

Gloria stopped and turned.

The guard stumbled and dropped his weapon, fumbling as he searched for it without taking his eyes off Snake.

"You have a death wish? Eyes!" Gloria hissed. The guard shifted his body and picked up his weapon.

"Enter the exit tunnel to your comrades on the third level," yelled Snake. Gloria realized then that Snake was helping her. She nodded.

The guard looked to have panicked and rushed through the tunnel, leaving. Snake grinned at Gloria and gave her the go-ahead wave. "A true coward to his race."

Gloria watched the guard until he turned the curve of the tunnel.

"Human, go before I get hungry," Snake said.

Gloria nodded and didn't say anything. She hurried to the incinerator and dumped the trash and paused a moment to watch it burn before she made her way to her cell. She went into her footlocker and took a pair of gray scrubs and tucked them under her arm.

She hurried back to Samantha's cell. The dimly lit tunnel hummed in a low tone. Gloria watched for the cameras and pressed the keypad and walked through the metal door.

7 RUBY

The clock on the wall showed just after midnight when the door opened.

"You're late. Did you get caught?"

"No, I had to clean up one of Banth's messes."

"You sure we won't be seen?"

"There's always the risk the drones will spot us. We just have to be quick and avert them."

I didn't know what to expect, but I was ready to find out about the Resistance for myself. Gloria lifted her smock and pulled out scrubs and handed them to me.

"Put these on."

"Lovely." It was better than the hospital gown I was used to wearing. I put on the scrubs in a hurry.

"Listen to me very carefully. You must block everything from your mind when you leave these walls. Do you understand? The drones will know you're gone. Think of a black piece of paper. Banth's remote viewing astral spies will find us if you don't. They'll report back to Banth and Ultra Seven. Do you understand?"

"Let's go."

Gloria put her thumb on the keypad. I watched, not seeing her do that before. The door opened.

"Only a few have clearance."

"Wait. What about the cameras? They'll see I am not here."

"We have thirty minutes while the cameras update and are offline."

"Okay, then. Let's do this."

We stood by the door, looking at each other like *Dumb and Dumber.* She paused.

"Are you ready?"

I nodded and followed Gloria through the door. She looked both ways before we proceeded down the tunnel.

The tunnel's low-strung lights reminded me of Area 51. About every twenty feet or so, a security camera pivoted towards the tunnel. My feet were bare, making walking a challenge, but I kept up with her. A small drone zoomed by.

"Samantha, duck!"

"Geez, it almost hit me in the head."

"Keep your head down!"

"Where are they coming from?"

"The central hub."

"We'll never make it!"

"Watch out, here comes another!" We ducked just in time.

I stayed close beside Gloria through the shafts.

The baleful stares of fellow captives stirred anxious thoughts. I took hold of Gloria's arm.

"What level is this?" I whispered.

"She pulled me onward and whispered, "The Hallway of Nightmares..."

"Seriously."

"Banth's favorite place."

Screams made me halt. "I don't know if I can do this."

"What's your alternative?"

"There isn't any. But that doesn't mean I have to like it, does it?"

"Understood."

"I don't have a good feeling about this... This is not a good idea at all. There has to be another way."

"There's no other way. We have no other choice."

"You're kidding, right?"

"Do you see me laughing?"

I froze, peering at a cell with a creature. Male, female, I couldn't tell; it glared at me with yellow avocado-colored eyes.

I pushed curiosity away as quickly as I could. Something about it made me want to stare back. As if hypnotized.

Gloria tugged on my arm.

"Don't rubberneck in the cells."

I turned away quickly.

"Why?" I whispered.

"They use mind control to draw you into their cell."

"Oh, hell no."

A bright greenish hue enclosed this section of the tunnels. I covered my eyes. One cell contained a multi-legged creature. Part animal, part human. Another knocked at the glass window at us.

I jumped away and stumbled back. "Are you sure this is the only way?"

Another pounded at the glass, glaring at me. Its face appeared almost human, but its backside resembled a spider's.

I locked eyes with the creature.

"Samantha, no!"

I felt numb, and my feet felt cemented to the ground. Gloria pulled me, breaking the trance.

The sound started out faint, then a little more, and then louder. There was no mistaking it. The noise of a weeping pup echoed. I stopped again.

This time, Gloria's persistence wore out. She tugged hard on my arm. "We must not stop!"

I broke free and began to follow the sound. "Wait a second. Listen!"

"Samantha, we can't stop. The drones will catch us. Let's keep going."

"No. Wait."

We trod to where we heard the whimpers coming from. I tiptoed, approaching a cell, and padded slowly until the glass window faced me.

"Oh, Gloria look." I stared in amazement.

"I wouldn't get too close. Some are hostile. Their appearance is deceiving."

"Oh my, it's a puppy. Like the kind, I had as a child. It has to be a German Shepherd!"

"Do you see how they use your memories to reel you in? Let's go!"

"It's so cute." I tapped the glass window, putting my head on it. "Come here, puppy."

"Be careful, Samantha, it could be one of Banth's experiments."

I touched the glass again, and the pup ran, heading for it and wagging its tail. I put my palm on the glass, and the puppy put its paw on the glass over my hand.

"Don't. This is very dangerous." Gloria looked over her shoulder. "We have to keep moving! Enough of this foolishness."

The puppy's tail wagged, jumping on the glass door.

"Look." I scooted down to get a better view of the puppy. The whimpering pup scratched the glass with its paws.

"Please. Let him out."

"Do you want to get us caught?"

"Please!"

Gloria put her thumb on the lock panel of the door. It opened. Out jumped the puppy into my arms, licking me and almost toppling me over onto the cement ground.

I peeked down at its adorable face. "It's eyes."

The pup's eyes began to glow a violet-red beam. "Did you see that? They're ruby red."

"Yes, now come on." Gloria scanned the area, her expression uneasy.

"Pet him. We have to name him. How about Ruby?"

"I know better than to take so much time. This is careless. The thirty-minute window for the cameras to be offline is approaching. We don't have much time now. We have to hurry."

I carried the pup, shielding it from the sounds of the tunnel. We moved at a fast pace through this part of the subway of Dulce. The darkened enclosure glowed with different eerie colors. We came to a fork where each side had large canisters with tubing going in and out of them. I tried to see what was coming out of them. We were just about to pass one. A liquid resembling egg yolk was being sucked through into a clear encasement. The closer we got, the more visible it became. I couldn't pry my eyes from the rudiments in tubular vats filled with the liquid and embryos.

"What is this place?" I whispered.

I stopped to gasp until Gloria pulled me away from the containers.

I held the pup tightly in my arms. Maybe to comfort me more than the furball.

"We have to hurry," Gloria whispered.

A drone whizzed by. Gloria and I cowered as we made our way down a side wall of the tunnel.

"This way to the elevator." She hit the elevator door, which opened into a darkened silo. Gloria pushed the number three, and up we went fast, reminding me of the elevator at Foster Ranch.

The puppy started to whimper like it knew we weren't supposed to be there.

The antechamber housed room after room like an open window studio. A few humans and hybrids wandered through the halls, probing me with curious eyes. We passed a young man with tousled hair. I gazed as if I knew him. The closer we got to the meeting place with the Resistance, the more the pup whimpered.

"Another human for the doctors to dissect, I see," a woman said, rushing toward us. She snickered, clawing the ground. I said nothing, turning my head.

"Is she human or alien?"

"Your guess is as good as mine."

"Shouldn't you know you been here forever."

"Try not to ogle," Gloria insisted.

"It's kind of hard when they're all glass cells."

I tighten my grip on the puppy while she wiggled in my arms, sensing my unease. As we approached the next windowed cell, I tried to shield my eyes. But I couldn't.

Two naked creatures were humping like wild boars on the cement ground of a cell. The one doing the humping studied me and grinned with fanged teeth, though not like a vampire at all. They were all fanged. I'd never seen anything like it, and I never wanted to. Ever—

"They're hybrids. A cross between a human and alien that didn't turn out very well. Another one of Banth's experiment that went wrong," Gloria said.

"I have to get out of here!"

I followed Gloria as she made the corner, almost running until the letter **B** came into view. She halted and composed herself.

"Is this it?"

She nodded and put her finger to her lips outside cell **B**. Cell **B** was quite large, not like the other cells.

Cardboard was fastened to the windows, shielding its view of the interior.

"This is a housing cell. The only time guards come up here is when Banth wants someone to tinker with."

"Who put up the cardboard?"

"We did... Some of the hybrids we just passed like to wander."

We sauntered and stopped outside the door. The lights were out, with only a flicker of a lantern glowing through the cardboard.

"Don't say a word. I'll do all the talking."

I rested my cheek on the pup.

My heart began to beat hard in my chest. I thought of Lucien. That first meeting when he put a rubber band on my wrist. How I wished I had it now. There's no place like home. There's no place like home. I guess it only works in the movies. I took a breath and held it in.

Gloria pressed her thumb on the keypad and peered at me carefully.

The door clicked, but it didn't vacuum open like the others.

"They destroyed some of the wiring, so they could make a barrier from intruders," Gloria said.

She knocked twice. A second of silence. Then a sound of wood rubbing against wood and the door opened.

"Don't say a word. And muzzle the dog," Gloria instructed.

I nodded and waited for the door to open. As it did, a tall, slender man stood holding a piece of plywood. I held my breath and followed Gloria into cell B.

8 THE RESISTANCE

Gloria entered first, hoping that Samantha had listened to her instructions. Inside were a dozen or so alien hybrids and humans, talking among themselves. Gloria had no trouble with the hybrids. They always seemed human to her. The only difference was a slant to their face or the way their ears pointed out almost like an elf's. Gloria remembered how Older, the oldest human abductee, told her the hybrids carved strange markings and tattoos on their skin to distinguish themselves from the others. They considered themselves the Clan of the Fallen. Some were as tall as seven feet, while others were small, almost dwarf-like.

The room quieted when Gloria and Samantha walked in. Their attention went right to Samantha. Tarragon, the tallest of the hybrids, who had tattoos on his face and arms, approached Gloria.

"Tarragon," she said.

Older, the shorter man with long, knotted blond hair and icy-blue eyes, acknowledged Gloria with a tip of his jaw. Scars edged his rough skin from the bottom of his lip to his brow and mimicked his arms.

"Older," Gloria said, embracing a gray-haired man with knotted hair.

"You know to never make this beast wait," Older said in Gloria's ear.

"It couldn't be helped," she whispered.

Noah, a younger lanky hybrid, stood close to Older.

Gloria kept watch on Samantha as she greeted the crowd. Some of the human and hybrid mixes were wearing tattered cutoff scrubs, others had fringes hanging like they were torn, individualizing them.

"Why did you bring this human here?" Tarragon said. His voice was calm but direct. "You're late as well."

"It couldn't be helped. I have good reason."

Older winked at Gloria, making her feel at ease a moment.

She acknowledged her dear friend with a short nod.

"You better have," Tarragon said.

"This human is Banth's new commodity. And I say that with the utmost respect." She turned, acknowledging Samantha.

The group eyeballed her as if she were an intruder. They glared. Some frowned. A few turned their backs, a common practice of the Fallen Clan.

Gloria had become accustomed to the mixture of alien and human DNA and made peace with the fact that some would never accept humans. She watched Samantha hold the wiggly pup beneath her grasp.

She feared they might take the animal from her and make it their dinner.

"We have to move quickly," Tarragon said.

"Only if we all agree," Older said.

"So, we all are going to help the cause?" Gloria exchanged glances between the older man and the taller human. She motioned for Samantha to come forward.

"Tarragon, this is Samantha," Gloria said.

Samantha nodded and gave a quick smile. She briefly looked at Tarragon's shirtless, tattooed chest with symbols and illegible writings and turned away quickly.

"Rek?" the other human hybrid said to Samantha.

She smiled.

Rek approached her.

Gloria quickly stood in front of Samantha protecting her. Rek gave Samantha the once-over without saying anything. The skin around his eyes appeared to be melted into his nose. Samantha lowered her gaze.

"I don't mean her harm," Rek said.

Gloria didn't say anything.

"You don't have to turn away, only if it scares

you," Rek said.

Samantha gazed at him again and give him a forced smile.

Gloria interrupted the two. Samantha didn't need to know how his face got that way. She knew all too well Banth was the cause.

"Banth's new project?" Tarragon said.

"She was taken from the Foster Clan."

"The Fosters?"

"The original six. Jordan Foster rescued them."

"Is she one of them?" Older said.

Gloria turned to Older. "No, she is human."

"You know of them!" Samantha said out loud.

"I have heard rumors," Older said.

"Samantha, Older is human like you and me. He was taken underground years ago."

"My family probably searched for years but gave up," Older said.

"Just like yours will do," Rek said with a smirk.

Noah, the young hybrid of the group, joined in.

"They all do. In time, yours will too."

"They won't," Samantha said.

"What did I tell you?" Gloria glared at Samantha.

"Are you here to educate me on the trials and tribulations of the life of new abductees or discuss the rebellion?" Tarragon said.

"Snake let me pass tonight... I've seen him. I swear to you, he is going to help."

"What makes you think so?" Older said.

"He's a myth!" shouted one of the humans in the crowd.

"No! I've seen him with my own eyes, I tell you! There were rumors he wasn't real, but he is real. He helped me."

"Why? Did he tempt you with his apple?"

Gloria walked up to Tarragon.

"They're attempting to sabotage the work on Levels Six and Perdition Seven. Like us, they secretly formed a small group with the same agenda as we," Rek said. "It has to be." He pushed his way between Noah and Gloria.

"So, it's true, then. The Reptilian Clan is going to help us," Tarragon said.

"It has to be," Rek said.

"How do you know this?" Older looked in Rek's direction.

"It doesn't matter if they are with us or not," Rek said.

Tarragon turned to everyone. "Are we going to do this or not?"

The crowd agreed.

Gloria raised her hand, attempting to quiet them. "When we attack, it has to be the right time. We have to avoid Removers and the Delta Force guards and especially Banth."

"We will never make it past the Removers," Older said, stepping forward.

"We will attack at the earliest. The flashgun is what will get us out," Tarragon insisted.

"How are we going to get one? Banth has them under lock and key."

Older gave Gloria a long gaze. She found comfort in his company. They were the two oldest humans in the Dulce underground base.

Tarragon walked over to his bunk. He studied the clock on the wall. "I have less than ten minutes before the camera comes online again."

He pulled his bunk away from the wall. Behind it was a small opening in the floor. He lifted a carved-out section and took out what resembled a flashlight with a black inverted lens. He held it high.

"The flashgun," he said with a broad smile.

Surprised, Gloria said, "Where did you get this?"

"Let's just say the cleanup crew in the Pit were a little careless," Tarragon said. He glided his hand on the weapon. "There are three phases to the gun. The marker is what will keep us alive. So, we all need to know how it works."

"There's not enough time to learn now," Gloria said.

"We better be quick learners, then." Older smiled at Gloria.

Tarragon moved his finger around the trigger. "If you position at this level," Tarragon placed his finger on a red knob, "it will create a temporary death."

"And I assure you, any doctor will concur it will

cause the person you shoot at to be paralyzed," replied Older.

Tarragon narrowed his eyes and raised a brow. "But know this... Whatever is left of them will linger on in a state of limbo."

"Their consciousness will remain in a non-death state." Older cleared his throat.

"How do you know this?" Gloria said.

"We've seen them. Older and I," Rek said.

Older acknowledged him. "We were working on the exhaust system when the cleanup crew was carrying the bodies away."

"The first phase stuns and may kill anyone with a weak heart." Tarragon peered at Older. "Phase two can levitate anything, even you." He turned to Noah, who seemed to be daydreaming.

His attention went to Rek, and he smiled. "No matter the weight."

Rek gawked at his protruding stomach.

Older chuckled.

"Phase three is serious business; it can paralyze anything or anyone that lives, don't matter if it's animals, humans, alien, or plant." He paused. "That will give us one to five hours to act. The alien or human will slowly revive. First, their bodily functions will begin to fade, and in a few minutes, they regain consciousness and then full awareness."

"We need more than one," Rek said.

"How will we get more?" Older said.

"The same way I got this one," Tarragon said. He observed them intently.

"Banth's Removers reprogram the brains of humans on Perdition Seven and plant false information using this weapon," Gloria said.

"I am aware," Tarragon said.

"And you want to take a chance on one of us to use it properly."

"I do."

"Well then, you're a fool. Have you been on Level Four? Have you seen the souls in the glass drawers? Moments of their lives play out like a video. Their memories, their existence. This is not a weapon to mess with, Tarragon."

"I've seen them."

"The flashgun in your hand is a highly dangerous weapon. In the wrong hands, there is no limit on the danger it could inflict."

"Gloria, do you have a better plan?"

"Do you?" Rek echoed Tarragon.

"No."

"Well, then, it's settled. We will attack at noon tomorrow human time."

"Do you think that's a wise move in the peak of the day?" said Older.

"Wait! I am not attacking." Samantha approached the others. "The Fosters will come! I know they will. I want to escape, but I am not joining your militia," Samantha bellowed.

"Not a militia, more like a coup d'état," Older said.

"Whatever!"

"Did anyone hear me ask this human if we wanted her to fight with us?" Tarragon said.

"I didn't, did you, Rek?" Noah said with a greasy smile.

"The Fosters are not going to save a human, especially one here," Tarragon said.

Gloria turned to Samantha. "No one is asking you to do anything. I thought you wanted a way out of here."

"I do, but..."

"You don't have much of a choice. It's this or nothing."

"I want to escape, but not like this. This is like the firefight, Gloria, the one I was talking about, and it was a massacre."

"You said some lived."

"Yes, but over a hundred died trying."

"If you don't come with us, you will spend the remainder of your life here underground in this horrible place. Do you understand?"

"Let her stay," Tarragon said.

"If she wants to. Who's to stop her?" Rek went to sit.

"Let her! If that's what she wants." Noah followed Rek to a table and picked up a hollowed-out drinking apparatus and drank from it.

Samantha watched with a grimace.

"There has to be a way to get a signal through the copper and boron walls and get word to the Fosters," Samantha asked with a brass tone.

"There's no way to break through it," Rek said.

"I basically have no choice, is that what you mean?" Samantha's eyes darted between them. No one spoke up. "So, I either go along with this plan or rot in here until I die." She rolled her eyes and hugged the pup close to her. Gloria empathized with her. She watched Samantha cower back into the wall, clutching the puppy in her arms. Gloria could almost feel her sadness. She turned away and finalized the details of the rebellion with Tarragon. She took the flashgun in hand while Tarragon ran through the phases while Samantha watched on.

9 BLUE HOLE

The desert air brushed against Lucien's tawny skin. His black locks blew from the afternoon breeze, leaving a single strand of gray to fall at his dark brow. He waved his hand, and the six-car garage door opened, blowing his hair from his face. He opened the Jeep's hatch, took a deep breath, and stared aimlessly into the trunk.

"Let me come with you," Eden said, taking hold of her brother's arm. He pulled away.

"Can't you just leave me be?"

"You're going to Dulce, aren't you?"

Her frown masked her flawless complexion. "You shouldn't go back there...I have to protect you."

"I think I can protect myself better than you. I'll be fine."

"No, you can fool Uncle, but you can't deceive me. I know you are hurting, I get that. If you're lucky, they'll kill you. And if they don't and they capture you— they won't let you leave. You'll spend eternity in the depths of the pit."

"Don't be so dramatic. And what could you do to help?" Lucien smiled at his sister.

He didn't want her or anyone else to get harmed because of him. At least not Eden, knowing the unpleasant history she and Sam had. Eden had a hard time being in the same room with Sam, let alone searching for her in some God-forsaken underground somewhere.

"You don't even know if Sam is at Dulce. Do you? It could be any number of the underground bases." Lucien turned to see his brother Michael, who had followed him.

"You know she's right, Brother. Sam could be at Perica, a large underground city near Page, Arizona, or any other half a dozen dwellings. What makes you so sure Banth has her there?"

"I just do! I have a strong feeling she's there," Lucien spat out.

He didn't care if his brothers and sister or Jordan thought it was a bad idea he was going. Lucien lifted a duffel bag full of weapons into the Jeep.

"Why bring all those? Do you have a secret army you're not telling us about?" Eden peered in the Jeep and stifled a laugh.

He picked up a duffel of water.

"You're exhausted. Wait until we know more about her whereabouts. Please, Lucien," Eden pleaded.

"I must save Samantha." He wiped tiny beads of

sweat from his brow.

"He's out of his mind."

He watched Michael glance at Eden.

"You do know I can read your mind." He chuckled under his breath.

"Go ahead and laugh. What you're doing is a death sentence," Michael said.

"I'd rather die saving her."

"Will you listen to your brother? Dulce is hell on Earth!" Eden said. "I will not let you die too."

Lucien ignored them. He gazed near the front lawn. Gabriel and Jordan headed for the garage.

"You're going to Dulce," Jordan said. His old face was worn and drained. He balanced his weight on his cane.

"Brother," Daniel said.

He was the one who saw the future. He settled next to his brother. Lucien didn't want to hear anything, including Daniel's prophecies.

"She's there. You're right."

"You're sure!" Lucien's voice raised like a boy reaching puberty into manhood.

"She is, but, Lucien, Dulce is a place of no return," Daniel said.

They stood watching Lucien gather the rest of his supplies in a moment and left the garage.
Lucien pondered what his siblings had said. His feet seemed to be guiding the way. He trod to the stables and saddled up Pepper, his favorite horse, and

reminisced about the day he and Sam took Pepper out for a gallop. It seemed like years ago, but it wasn't that long ago. The horse began to gallop hard, covering the length of the Foster Ranch.

He climbed down from the majestic animal and stood to gaze over the ranch. What if Sam was dead? Or what if she lived after Banth did what he wanted to do to her? Would she ever be the same once she was underground at Dulce?

He fought to shut off the dark thoughts that his sister and brothers were flooding his mind with. He tried to feel her.

He made up his mind he would leave at sundown with or without his family's blessing.

Lucien thought a moment before putting his foot in Pepper's stirrups, he lightly pulled on the reins, and turned back to the ranch not bothering to tell his family he was leaving. All he could think of was Samantha.

He swung his leg over the saddle and dismounted and walked Pepper back to the stable. Out of nowhere, a white feather glided in front of him. He held out his palm, as it landed softly. He picked it up.

"Where are you, Sam?" he said out loud and trod back to the Jeep.

He was just about to close the hatch of the Jeep when a black Navigator pulled up. Out stepped Joe Hunter.

Lucien remembered the last time he'd seen Sam's dad, who had been upset during their previous encounter. Joe stomped up the driveway with flared nostrils. "Where's my daughter?" His brow was furrowed.

"Mr. Hunter, Sam is..." For the first time in his life, he was at a loss for words.

"I got a call from Nathan Moore a while back. He said Sammy was being detained by the FBI! She was supposed to come home. That was a month ago! The last I heard, she was coming home after the fire at Oakridge Estates."

"If you were so concerned, why now? Where were you a month ago?" Lucien turned his back to Joe.

Joe went for his shoulder.

"Foster! Look at me. I don't know what you are or what you're involved in, and frankly, I don't care. I just want my daughter back safe at home!" Joe's voice echoed through Corona's tobosa grass.

Lucien turned to face Joe. His expression was emotionless, just like the alien DNA that ran through his veins. "I'm not involved in anything. Mr. Hunter, do you understand?" Lucien's eyes glowed neon green. "Sam is visiting friends. She will be home soon. You are happy that she finally is enjoying her life. Do you understand?"

Like a robot, Joe nodded yes.

"Joe, where is Sam?"

"Sam is visiting with friends."

"Good. Now get in your car and go home. Sam is on vacation. Don't worry. I will call you when she's going to come back," Lucien said. His eyes returned to normal. "It was nice seeing you, Mr. Hunter."

"Likewise, Lucien. Have a good day." Joe fumbled with his car keys and got into his vehicle and grimaced.

Lucien watched him pull away. Just as Joe was leaving, Gabe came sprinting out the front door of the ranch.

"Lucien! It's Dejaha Zoris —Sam's at Dulce!"

"Daniel's right!" A spark of hope lit up Lucien's face.

"No doubt about it." Gabe waved his hand, and a picture of Dejaha Zoris materialized in front of the brothers on a virtual computer.

"Samantha Hunter is being held at Dulce we know that for sure. Banth has gone too far this time. We don't have all the intel yet, and the Division is falling apart. There's word there's a vessel approaching, and it could be the Morians. Something brewing. There's some speculation most likely a battle between the Originals, Mutants and the Morians for earth. The 'No Whites', Banth's hybrid cell, has released another virus. This one is sure to raise havoc on the human population, unlike the one in March. Every man and woman on Earth will be infected within days. The Moirans thought they had destroyed the serpentine race and their henchman at Dulce. Whoever is in charge at Dulce be it Banth or not they want to claim Earth as his own. They are set on killing every human being. Most of the hybrids on Earth have gone into hiding, branching out from Dulce, Arizona, Colorado, and Alaskan underground cities. As soon as the virus destroys all human life, they will rise above; until then," Dejaha Zoris said.

"You sure about this virus?" Lucien said with a wrinkled brow. Beads of sweat began to form on his forehead. He studied his brother with uncertainty.

"The alliance," Gabe said.

"We haven't heard anything."

"The underground is preparing. Of course, we will take all precautions to defend ourselves against the underground dwellers— if we see they will not live peacefully above the ground."

"Who told you about the virus?" Lucien demanded.

"The President of the United States."

"That doesn't make any sense, unless..."

"The president? He's—" Gabe shook his head in disbelief.

"I don't believe it! He looks human, if he is a Moiran why would they want to kill every human being on this planet? They're a peaceful race."

"Peaceful? Lucien, you were mistaken. The Moirans are the deadliest race when it comes to finding a new planet to survive on. They have been dying for the last decade. They may be working with Banth."

"Remember the Ark. You saw what happened then," said Dejaha Zoris.

"Why are you talking about a campfire story someone made up in a cave for?"

"It's just an analogy," Eden quickly stated.

"This is a bunch of bull! It must be a mistake. All the journals and logs Jordan saved for us were lies."

"Why would uncle make it up? Why would he tell us the 'Moirans' were peaceful," Lucien said telepathically to Gabe.

"I am sorry to have been the one to enlighten you. This was just a courtesy call. If I were you, I would get your human female while there's anything left of her. Dulce was never a fun place to be at, but now it's the deadliest time to be there, with a vessel approaching carrying Moirans. The residence of the compound is going to be on alert." The transmission was gone.

Lucien and Gabe stood there a moment without saying a word, just reading each other's thoughts. "I don't believe Jordan would have lied to us all this time."

Lucien opened the Jeep's door and sat down inside.

"He did it for a reason, Brother. It's because he

wanted us to believe we were good and not like them. At least you."

"What's that supposed to mean. Like me?" Lucien snarled at his brother.

"It came out wrong, Brother is all." Gabe held the Jeep's door, peering down at Lucien.

"If we are the same and have the same genes, then why aren't we as evil as they are?" Lucien said, starting the Jeep.

"Zoris never stated that they were evil. They are in survival mode."

"So, kill innocent humans so they can live?"

"You have to stop trying to save every creature." Lucien raked his hands through his hair.

"I just don't understand." He paused.

"I got to go. I have to find Sam before they kill her."

"Let me go, I can shift and be there in an hour."

"No. I have to do this myself."

"There's no way in there. It's entirely encased with copper and boron," Gabe said.

Michael opened the front door to the ranch. He stood a moment watching and hurriedly joined the conversation. Lucien closed the Jeep's door before Michael approached him.

"It's a death wish, Brother," Michael said.

"I'll go by the Blue Hole. From the cavern, through the tunnels. No one will see me."

"No, it's too risky!"

"Don't worry." Lucien started the Jeep.

"I'm coming," Michael said.

"No."

"I don't want to lose another brother," Michael said, leaning in the Jeep.

"I need you here to see after Jordan."

"Eden can."

"No!"

"Dammit, Lucien, you're so bull-headed." Michael sighed. "If you're going to try and be a savior again, you'll need to take this with you." Michael reached into his pocket and took out a small black box. Inside were two capsules. "Take it before you enter Dulce. Otherwise, all your abilities will be compromised. The dwelling is coated with boron and copper like I said."

Lucien took the box and tightened his grip within his palm. "Thank you."

"You sure about this, Brother?"

Lucien didn't wait to give Michael an answer. He peeled out the driveway in reverse. All he could think of was Sam and choking the life out of Banth.

He turned up the volume on the Jeep's GPS.

"Turn right onto Old Desert Road. Two hours to your destination. The Blue Hole is east of Albuquerque on old Route 66 in Santa Rosa. It's known as the 'City of Natural Lakes.'"

Lucien rehearsed over and over in his mind how he was going to kill Banth. He glanced at the clock on the dash. It was just before nightfall. The New Mexico sky was sun-streaked with colors of amber and mango over the horizon. He slowed down when he saw the first sign reading "The Blue Hole."

He turned the wheel when he eyed three boys hanging out over the edge of the circular pond of water, drinking.

The Jeep's headlights reflected off one of the kid's eyes as Lucien pulled up to the Blue Hole.

He turned off the engine and sat a moment while his demeanor changed. He pushed "nice" Lucien aside before stepping out of the Jeep.

A smile was on his face as he walked in the direction of the boys in a relaxed manner.

The closer he got, laughter filled the chilled evening until the group straightened themselves up to glare at the stranger approaching them.

One of the awkward boys stood and walked up to Lucien. "Dude, you're not invited."

Lucien continued to approach, unshaken. "Really? I was—a bit thirsty."

"Bro, I said this is a private party."

"I'm warning you," a fat teen said at the water's edge with fists clenched. He glared at Lucien with his nostrils flared and took his beer can and threw it at Lucien's feet. Lucien stopped and smiled at the can and picked it up.

"Littering is a crime in New Mexico."

Lucien pitched the can in the trash can and

continued to approach the boys, but this time, his eyes glowed a neon green color. And with a smooth voice, he said, "I think you've had enough to drink."

The teen dropped his hands. The other two teens stood at full tilt.

Lucien turned to them. "Didn't your mommy teach you littering is wrong?" The boy dropped the can and went limp. "Didn't I just say littering was a crime? Now pick it up." The boy bent over and picked up the can like a robot. A wet spot began to appear on the boy's jeans.

"What the— hell did you do to him? He pissed himself.!"

Lucien stared at them. The other two boys started to advance. Lucien held up his hand in their direction.

The boys stopped and went limp.

"Boys, listen carefully to what I am going to say. Pick up your beer cans and get in your cars and leave and never say a word to anyone about what just happened. Do you understand?"

The boys nodded. They picked up all the beer cans and dumped them in the trash while Lucien watched.

"Now get in your cars and go bye-bye."

The boys walked to their cars and got in. Lucien waved. "Remember to give a hoot, don't pollute."

Once in their cars, they rubbed their faces, sharing expressions of terror. They started their vehicles and peeled away onto the highway.

Lucien chuckled for a moment, watching them skedaddle liked the scared children they were.

He hated being alien, but it did come in handy at times. He strode near the body of water and picked up the teens' scuba gear and tossed it in the trashcan. Lucien gazed down at the blue water of the Blue Hole, an eighty-foot-deep artesian spring fed from an underwater aquifer. Ripples of clear water glistened in front of him. Looks were deceiving. It was a deadly precursor to the depths of hell, he thought. He looked down at his boots and was about to take them off. And decided not to. He sighed, thinking of Sam one last time before diving. He missed everything about her, her soft ivory skin, even her quirky thoughts.

The last of the daylight splashed indigo across the horizon. He paused a moment and peered out into the evening air. A soft breeze rustled through his hair. It was now or never, he thought. He stepped forward onto the edge. He took another breath, clearing his lungs, and dived into the pool of blue water.

Lucien swam deep within the Blue Hole, deeper and deeper until the water became dark and frigid. The bottom of the cave-like structure unknown to anyone came into sight. The secret entrance to Dulce.

A rocky underpass came into view. Lucien could

see the structure begin to change. One last dive upward was what it would take to get to the surface of the cave. He plunged until his head broke through the water. It wasn't a problem for him to stay under water. One of his abilities was to conserve oxygen. The sodium chloride in the ocean water actually helped him stay under water longer.

A rush of air filled his lungs as he scanned the murky, rocky, cold hollow. Icicle-like stalactites hung from the ceiling. His eyes glowed, lighting up the interior dampness with his alien eyes. He swam until he came to a rock ledge.

He scanned the area as he moved with caution, pulling himself out of the water, dripping. He inspected the underwater sinkhole at several tunnels. He shook off the water from his clothes and boots almost like a dog.

He thought for a moment, trying to get a vibration of psychic energy from Sam. He closed his eyes and meditated. Still nothing.

10 BONE MARROW

"Put the mutt in its cage," Gloria said.

"But I want to keep it."

"The lab workers will see that it's gone and will hunt it down."

"But—"

"If they find it, they will serve it to the aliens for dinner on Perdition Seven."

Banth's security unit usually put the hybrids down if they left their cells. I couldn't let that happen to Ruby.

I did what Gloria asked and closed Ruby's crate.

To tell the truth, I hated when Gloria left me. I watched her leave through the deserted hallway to the main tunnel. The only light on the ceiling flickered, and then her image faded. I turned around and looked at the gray cell. This was my new home. I had to go along with Tarragon's plan. What could go wrong? I could get killed? It's not like that ever stopped me before. Death was a better option than this place.

Why was this happening to me? I kept telling

myself this was a nightmare, and I would wake up any minute. I didn't wake up. It was real. Lucien was dead. No one was searching for me.

My dad must think I'm dead for sure. Cassiel, Eden, Michael, all gone. I'd be trapped down here like Gloria forever if the Resistance didn't win. Gloria was right. They were my only hope out of here.

I crawled back in my bunk and held the blankets up to my chin. I felt like I was drowning in water. I had no rubber band to snap and bring me back to a safe place. Maybe if I screamed loudly, they would give me something to dull the pain in my heart.

"It's been hours since Gloria left. What if she is never coming back?"

God help me. I prayed. I can't remember any prayers. I thought back to when I was a little girl at Sunday school.

"Father Abram...no. Our Father in Heaven, hallowed be your name. I can't remember. Dear God, help," I said out loud with tears stinging my eyes. I couldn't stand it. I got up. "Help me! Somebody! Anybody! Help! Help!"

"She's calling out to God. Do you hear the human? There is no god here," the voice behind the door said.

"Let me out!"

I ran over to the metal door and pounded on it. The cell was windowed, but I couldn't see out. Only the guards could see in.

I fell to the cold floor, crying. I lay in a fetal position, sobbing for what seemed like hours. A loud voice behind the door woke me.

"Human up, up." The door opened.

"Stop!"

Someone pulled me by the hair and dragged me to the cot. I opened my eyes.

A tall alien hybrid with translucent skin and huge eyes took my arms and shackled them to the side of the bed.

"What are you doing? Stop! I'm sorry. I promise I won't scream again!"

He ignored my plea and took my legs and shackled them too. The door opened. Gloria came rushing in.

"Gloria, please help me!" I turned to see one alien take out a huge needle. "Stop them! No. No, please."

I squirmed on the bed, trying to free myself.

"What're you doing with this human?" Gloria asked.

"Banth wants another blood sample!" the huge alien with a gray cast to his face said.

"For what? He's already done that?"

Gloria pushed her way in my direction.

"Stand down, human, or you're going to solitary."

"You don't have the authority! I said blood was

already taken."

"It's ordered."

Gloria took my hand. I could tell by her expression she could not stop whatever they had planned for me.

"Samantha, let them take the sample."

"Why! What do they want it for?"

"It's customary. They do it to all the abductees," the creature said.

"But they already did one!"

I watched them wrap a band around my arm tightly. I cringed when the needle broke the skin. I held in my scream.

Gloria watched on with pleading eyes.

The guard undid the band and released my arms and legs and left with his sample. I rubbed my arm hard where they had poked me.

The room suddenly got cold. Gloria went over to the window trying to see out. She didn't say anything at first and then came close.

"What's with the blood?" I asked.

"Not sure. They usually aren't that quick." She rubbed her forehead. "It may be because..." She stopped.

"What?"

"There's a human baby...at least I think its human by its appearance. It's in the infirmary. Banth is watching over it. I believe they are doing experiments on it."

"Oh, my God...that's horrible. They stole someone's baby."

"Samantha, you're not the only human here."

"Of course, I wouldn't be. I should know better."

"The baby's dying. And they need bone marrow to save it," Gloria said.

"Bone marrow?" I rubbed my arm. "They're testing my blood to see if it's a match!"

"Have you made your decision about the rebellion?"

"I don't want to be involved in your war. I just want a way out. A baby...."

"Yes."

"It seems like he is trying to save it, not hurt it."

"They will keep experimenting on the baby and who knows how many they have. Do you see why we must go along with the Resistance? If we don't—"

"This is not my circus, not my monkeys."

"Monkeys?"

"Never mind. I guess you're not Polish."

She rolled her eyes.

"It's just a Polish proverb, you know? An expression. I don't care what's going on here. I just want out!"

She still seemed confused.

"Jesus, Gloria, it's not my problem!"

"So, you don't care about them dissecting an infant or experimenting with the pup."

"You're trying to make me feel guilty. Is that

your tactic to make me cave?"

"I can't help how you feel." She just stood there gawking at me.

"If I help...do you think we can get to the baby and save it?"

"We can try."

"Then I will help get this baby to a real doctor."

"I will get word to Tarragon." Gloria smiled.

The door opened. Two of Banth's guards and a lab worker bolted in, knocking Gloria out of the way.

Raul Roman came in, geared up in blue scrubs.

One of the guards picked me up and threw me on the cot.

"Ugh! What are you doing!"

"Easy, boys. Banth doesn't want this one hurt."

I squeezed my eyes shut a second and opened them. I should have kept them closed, because the tall alien hybrids with translucent skin and enormous eyes made me want to throw up. Olive-colored slime oozed from their glowing golden eyes. I turned my head for fear it would drip on my face. They took my arms and shackled them tight.

"Stop! You're hurting me!"

"Quiet, human," the one at my feet said.

"Bone marrow," the other alien said.

"You couldn't have had time to test her blood!" Gloria said fast.

"We have the most up-to-date lab. You know that Gloria," Banth replied, walking through the sliding doors.

Raul Roman stepped closer. "You sure about this?" He turned to face Banth.

"Why would you even ask such a stupid question?"

"Just thought—"

"You're an idiot. Why wouldn't I be? Sometimes I wonder where your loyalty lies!" Raul Roman took a needle from a caddy an alien brought in.

He held it high in the air. For a moment, I almost saw concern in his eyes right before he poked me with it.

The needle went deep into my skin. "Owww! You are hurting me."

The alien who had brought the caddy in wheeled a gurney. "On two," they said, lifting me on it.

"Okay, then, take her to the lab," Banth said. He gazed at me and smiled. "No worries, Samantha, you will be okay... It will only hurt a lot."

The alien said nothing as he pushed me out of the room down the hall. Everything was moving slowly. The walls were coming down all around.

"What did they give me? I feel weird."

"Not sure. I'm guessing they don't want you moving around too much. Some sort of a muscle relaxer."

"Gloria," I said in a whisper. "Where are they taking me?"

She didn't reply.

They rolled me into a brightly lit room.

The room where they took me appeared to be sterile. The ceiling had spotlights and chipped white paint. White tile decorated the side walls. The smell of antiseptic and bleach burned my nose.

The two alien guards lifted me off the gurney onto a surgical table.

Gloria stood by my side as the aliens pushed me over to my left side and shackled me to the bed rail. Then Raul Roman put a sheet over me, so just my hip was exposed. I couldn't see what they were doing, but I felt their icy touch even with gloved hands. I turned my head, trying to see. Unfortunately, every time I did, they held my head still.

My heart pounded hard in my chest, and I could feel sweat bead across my brow.

"Aren't you going to give her something for the pain?" I heard Gloria say.

"We're out. Not a new supply until next week," Raul Roman said. I could see his gaze meet Gloria's.

"What are you planning to do with her?"

"Gloria! Gloria, what are they doing!" I said.

"He wants her bone marrow, and then your bet is as good as mine," Raul Roman said calmly.

Gloria took my hand, and the aliens held me still.

"This is inhumane."

"How do you think they did it years ago?" Raul

Roman replied.

"How—would—she know? She's been here—all her life," I said through gritted teeth.

"Samantha, don't..."

"Like savages, they kept you here. And you want me to keep quiet!"

I felt a rush of coldness, and then the pain. I turned my head again and saw a large syringe filled with a dark-colored substance.

They were taking my bone marrow.

"I hope you rot in hell," I said through the pain.

"We're already there," Raul Roman said.

I lay there crying. My tears fell like raging rapids streaming down my face. I wanted to die. I closed my eyes, wishing I was dreaming, but the seething pain proved otherwise. Raul Roman covered the needle hole in my hip and unshackled me from the bed rail.

"It's going to hurt there for a while."

Raul Roman pushed the matted tear-drenched hair from my face. "Whatever you do, don't get too comfortable."

"I don't see that ever happening."

He frowned and locked eyes with me, and for an instant, I almost saw a hint of humanity. They left me alone with Gloria.

She pulled up a swivel chair close to me. "It has to be for the baby I saw."

"I thought Banth just wanted to make his super alien. Why is this baby so important?"

"I don't know." She glanced at the clock on the wall. "We have to go. Can you walk?" Gloria said with determination in her voice. She gazed at the door. "Can you?" she said.

"I think I can. Why?" I said taking in a breath. "Is it time? Are they going to rebel?"

"I don't know. But you are not safe here now."

"Why?"

"They got what they wanted."

"They're going to kill me, aren't they?" She didn't answer.

Sirens sounded.

"We have to get out of here."

"What's happening?"

"Once it starts, the tunnels will be filled with the Delta Force soldiers. The Ultras and who knows which other aliens are working on Banth's behalf. We only have a few minutes before they come back for you. Banth got what he wanted. He will most likely kill you," Gloria said, studying the camera.

"Why? I thought he wanted my eggs to use Lucien's DNA to make super soldiers?"

Gloria helped me off the table.

"He got what he wanted from you. Your DNA. He doesn't need your eggs anymore."

"What's he going to do—clone me?"

"Much more. Now let's go. Tarragon will hide you until it's safe."

We went out the sliding metal doors.

I halted in my steps. A sudden wave of nausea swept over me.

"I'm not sure I trust you. Tell me what you meant by 'much more'!"

"You want to die?" Gloria stared.

"Eventually, I hope, but not here. Like this."

"Then move."

We hurried through the narrow hallway. A high-pitched cry echoed.

"Do you hear that?"

Gloria locked eyes with me.

"It's a baby," I whispered.

She kept scanning ahead. "Keep going."

"Gloria, the baby."

"There are all kinds of sounds here deep within the levels. You must get them out of your mind."

"How much further?"

"We are near the level of the Elder Clan."

The tunnel became narrower. The lights flickered.

Gloria let out a moan. The lines of her face hardened as she led me to a dark cell.

It was the same area we came before, but it looked different. The strange aliens were gone, the cells empty.

Gloria paused and held out her arm to stop me going any further. "Something isn't right."

"You're right. They've gone."

"Tarragon's cell is empty. We're too late," she

said.

Gloria left my side. She pushed his bunk away and lifted the small piece of tile. She turned to stare at me.

"They're not here."

She searched a part of the wall of another section.

"All of the weapons they were storing. They're gone," Gloria said, composed.

I bent over in pain.

"We were too long."

"Augh…it's not like we could help it."

"We have nothing to defend ourselves with." Gloria grimaced.

"What are we going to do?"

"We have to go to the upper levels. They must be heading there. But I don't think it's safe for you, not like this."

"I don't want to go back to my cell!"

She raised an eyebrow. "I think it's best I bring you back to the infirmary."

I shook my head no. "You're kidding? After that lecture, you just gave me about Banth wanting me dead? And you want to send me back!"

"You're too weak."

"I am fine. I can make it."

"You will hold me back."

"Please—don't leave me there. They'll do more experiments. You said Banth will kill me."

There was a second of silence. "You can stay here. It will be the safest place for you. Once I know where Tarragon and the others have gone, we will come for you. I promise."

"You going to leave me here. You're like an emotional sniper. You know that?"

"I've waited so long. This is my only chance at freedom. Even if it's for a little while."

I studied Gloria's expression. I didn't even want to imagine what they did to her all these years.

"It will be the safest for you. They won't come here. They're sleeping. I can assure you. I'll send Rek and Noah for you!"

I stood there at the entrance while Gloria surveyed the tunnel, then me. "You will be all right."

"Why do I get the feeling you are double-thinking everything?"

"No.... I'm not. I just don't know for sure where they went."

Gloria turned and left. I watched the metal door close.

I was left with a chill down my back. I picked up the board that Tarragon used to block the entrance and held it in my arms as I turned and inspected the room. It was filthy but better than my cell. I climbed on a cot and stared at the blank walls. The motion sensor turned on, dimming the lights.

The noise of the lights going dim made me shudder. I'd never felt more alone in my entire life.

I rubbed my hip where the needle poked me and rolled on my side, trying to get comfortable. I lay there staring into the blackness, focusing on a light on the ceiling. While I kept staring, the light blew out. I sat up, almost springing to my feet. My nerves were on overdrive. I studied a broken camera that was hanging by wires. Before I knew it, it was moving by itself.

I stopped concentrating, and the camera stopped moving. I studied it again, this time with more concentration. The camera did a 360. Flabbergasted, I thought a moment. Just like the Fosters, my thoughts could move objects. I stood and started moving anything not nailed down. I lifted my hands, and the blanket flew off the bed. The chair tumbled over! The table where Rek had been sitting tipped. I laughed out loud. The cup that Rek had been drinking from tipped over, spilling the liquid out.

I was becoming like Lucien. How could this be? I thought about when he told me he gave me his blood. How my eyes changed colors and my hair. I was becoming alien. Not only could I see Finn, but I could also move things with my mind.

His DNA mixed with mine. That must be it.

I kept this up for hours until exhaustion swept over me. I climbed back on the cot, fell asleep, and began to dream. Banth had a baby in his arms. He dunked it in a basin of water, drowning it. The baby was a newborn and screaming. I could hear the baby's cries get louder and louder until I woke with a start. Sweat covered me top to bottom. I lay back down and tried to sleep. Another loud wail. My eyes shot open. It was quiet again. I waited. Another long cry. I sat up and hugged the wooden board, listening to the whimpering until the sound muted. I listened to the silence.

The sounds came again. Then it changed. Ruby, I thought. I stood and walked over to the metal door. If I had Lucien's DNA in my cells, then I could open this door. Right? I concentrated and focused until I could almost feel my eyes glowing. I went over to my reflection in a broken mirror on the wall. I smiled at the reflection staring back at me. My eyes were neon green just like Lucien's would get.

I first tried just using my mind without my hand, and nothing happened. Then I tried with both my hand and my mind, and the door inched open. I smiled to myself and tried again.

"Try both, Sam."

"Finn, is that you?" I turned to my right.

"The camera's light is child's play."

I turned to my left.

And right in front of me, inches away, was Finn, sporting a broad smile. "Yep, it's me."

My smile met his.

"You don't know how glad I am to see you," I said.

"Open it all the way."

"It's too heavy."

"It would be if you were human. But you're not anymore." Finn laughed. "You're a mixture of what every scientist, atomist, and physicist is searching for. You—Sam." Finn laughed again "You're the missing link to the universe."

He approached me and held out his hand. "Go ahead, touch me. It's really me." I winced a moment and plunged into his arms.

I thought I'd never see you again after the highway." We hugged. "I felt so alone here."

"I thought I heard a baby cry. There's a baby in a nursery that's ill. Banth took some bone marrow from me to keep it alive. But it's Ruby, the little German shepherd hybrid. She's been crying for hours. I need to find her. Come with me," I said excitedly, taking his hand.

"Let's go find your pup!"

I threw the board. The door opened.

The lights overhead flickered. I paused and gazed at tunnels—too many options. I pondered. My heart raced in my chest.

"Sam, this way," he said.

I followed Finn down a hallway resembling a hospital ward. Every room we passed was filled with hybrids of every kind.

"Why are they so quiet? It's like their tongues were removed."

"Do you really want to find out?"

He took my arm. I followed him down to a dimly lit lab with blue lighting. He stopped and scanned the area.

"We have to go back!" he said.

"No! Can't you hear it?" I turned around, still hearing the muffled sirens. "Do you hear that!"

Finn listened.

The whimpering started again. "It's Ruby."

"That's no puppy."

"Maybe it's more than one."

I raced until the cries were overbearing. I stopped and listened, trying to narrow down where the screams were coming from. I slowed my pace to a fast walk. The sounds got closer. My heart pounded, scared of what I might find. I turned the corner and approached a dark glass enclosure. The light coming from the room cast a greenish hue. I prayed they didn't hurt Ruby.

I slowed my pace as I came closer to the chamber. Fluorescent lights were hanging from the ceiling. A dozen incubators lined the small room. Each radiated a neon lime color with a purring sound like a content cat. There were babies in the incubators. Infants. At a snail's pace, I padded to each crying baby.

"Where did they all come from?" I said, pausing at each tiny, living, breathing baby. They looked human, perfect in every way.

Gazing at the side walls, I saw embryos in

capsules that mimicked wombs. The humming echoed through the tunnel.

"Sam, I don't think you should be here."

"What is this place!"

"Doesn't seem like your puppy is here."

Peeps echoed in the makeshift nursery. One tiny baby's shriek caught my attention, its face red from crying.

"You poor thing."

I scooped the infant into my arms. Its sweet scent calmed my nerves. I cuddled the baby, soothing it close to my chest. Together we calmed each other. Instantly, the baby stopped crying. A piercing siren blasted.

"We have to get out of here," I said.

I held the infant tight against my chest as the lights came on and the sirens blared. I squinted. The baby wailed.

"Too late," Finn yelled over the siren.

Before I knew it, they-they because I never saw anything so ghastly before—were upon us. I held my breath from the urine odor coming from them. Their skin oozed a slimy yellow sheen.

What I was warned about was right in front of me. These had to be the Removers. I really wasn't in the mood to find out what exactly they removed, but I had a pretty good idea. Gloria had said this group of aliens were as evil as they got. I could almost hear her voice telling me to run!

They got their kicks by playing a game with the humans, sort of like "it," and I was it. I stood gawking at them straight in the eyes. My heart pumped hard, but now I had a newfound confidence. My DNA wasn't from this world anymore. I was not quite a hybrid, but more. My cells were changing and multiplying into something I wasn't sure of yet. My body, my flesh, my brain were evolving into a new species of alien. I stared at the Remover.

"Run, human," he said, challenging me. He gave me a half smile, showing long, razor-sharp teeth that were much too large for its gray oval head.

"Finn, what should I do?"

He didn't answer. "Finn?" Where did he go? "Thanks for leaving me now," I said sarcastically.

"Human, you have my snack in your arms," the Remover said with slime hanging on its teeth like a dog after a long run. "You're it."

I sank down and held the baby tight. The Removers stepped closer. I backed up until I cowered into the corner.

"We will give you a head start. One, two, three. Human, don't you know the rules of the game?"

I thought a moment. "It doesn't seem fair, you are so tall and all. Your legs are longer than mine." I watched them look over at each other, thinking.

The one said to the other, "The human has a point." The one Remover glared at his counterpart.

"She does have a point," he said, lifting a long, bird-like leg. "Okay then, human, we will give you a longer head start."

"I'm not really dressed for a race."

"One, two, three."

My only option was to run. Run as fast as I could. It was three against one—well, the baby didn't count. I spun in the opposite direction out the glass door and ran through the dimly lit hallway. It was still in the middle of the night, and most of the lab workers were gone. I raced like the devil himself was behind me. I could hear the Removers laughing as they mocked me with their evil rhymes.

"Run, run, human, if you can."

"We will remove your heart with our hands," the other one said.

I tried to stifle the baby's cries while I ran. I had to find my way to Gloria and the Resistance while I still had half a chance of survival. I gazed down at the crying infant in my arms. This wasn't happening.

I heard a siren and red flashing lights. I came to a narrow opening. There were two exits but to where? I looked down, searching for another way out. My gut was telling me to hide, but where?

"Wait!"

I stopped in my tracks.

I rubbed my eyes with my free hand.

"Sam, this way."

Cassiel. "You're dead."

"And tell me something I don't already know!"

"Is it really you?" I smiled rushing to him. A wave of relief swept over me. I wanted to touch him to see if he was real. I tightened my grip on the baby and looked down as it slept in my arms.

Cassiel grimaced.

"You have to follow me. Now! I'm the only help you have," Cassiel said in a low, rushed voice.

"You saw them. Tell me you saw them!"

"Saw what?" Cassiel said.

"The embryos. They're babies, human babies alive in jars!"

"Sam, this place makes you see what you want." He gazed at the baby.

"There're more?"

He studied the infant I was holding.

I frowned and nodded.

"Then I have to get you out of here and quick."

"I guess this is my new reality. Seeing dead people."

"Take it or leave it. I'm all you got right now."

He glanced at the baby but didn't say anything. He led me through a passageway beyond the wall. The low ceiling was encased in spiderwebs, and rodents covered the ground. I followed him. "There's no place like home. There's no place like home."

"Keep telling yourself that."

"Ohhh, this is so gross." I stepped over rodents.

One touched my foot. "Ughhh. Get me out of here. What I would do for a pair of shoes right now!"

His eyes and mine lit the way. I wasn't sure where we were going, but I wanted him to take me away to a secret place. I wanted to escape and find Lucien and go somewhere. I could hear the Removers laughing as they mocked me with their evil rhymes some more. I tried to stifle the baby's cries while I ran. I had to find my way to Gloria.

A spotlight lit up the interior of the underground tunnel and with it Cassiel. He was gone with the light. I could see The Removers staring me down.

I smiled. "Okay," I said and raised my hand, and the sliding door opened. I fled down the unlit corridor of the Dulce underground.

I breathed in lungsful of stale recycled air, passing one after another glass cell holding every conceivable combination of alien and human DNA. A thin sheen of cold sweat beaded on my skin. I halted in my tracks when I heard crying. I listened. It wasn't Ruby. I listened again. Was I running in circles?

"Sam! This way."

I spun around. Cassiel.

"It's too dangerous," the apparition said. "Area Fifty-one is nothing compared to this." I scanned the ghostly image.

"Cassiel, is Lucien..." I said calmly.

"Alive. But you're not going to be if you don't get

somewhere safe!"

"He is?"

"Lucien's alive, Sam."

Relief washed over my face. I wanted to cry and laugh at the same time. "Where is he?" I whispered. As much as I wanted to stay and chitchat with Cassiel, my heart was pumping in my chest. I had to get to Gloria.

The lights blared. I tried to squint when in front of me appeared two tall creatures and Banth.

"Take the infant."

"No! You can't have him," I screamed.

Banth's foot soldier pulled the infant from my arms. I struggled to take him back.

"Don't hurt him!"

11 INTRUDER

Lucien studied the stalactite hanging from the ceiling of the dark, damp cave and then the length of the grotto for some entrance into the tunnels.

He touched the surface of the rocky wall, almost caressing the ancient dwelling until he saw a split in the wall with an outline of an entrance within the rock. He let his hand hover over the rock until the pillar vanished in front of him.

He backed away until it opened and entered the threshold with caution. The decrease in temperature made him shiver.

The ceiling dropped with just enough room for him to walk upright. He noticed a strong sulfur smell the deeper he went. He increased his pace, shuffling through the unfamiliar subterranean passages of Dulce.

His thoughts kept going back to Sam. He regretted going against Cassiel's wishes when he healed her.

He should have let her die rather than succumb to this place. He knew death was a better option than what lay within the levels at Dulce.

The more he traveled the depths of the tunnel,

the narrower it got. As he continued through, remnants of clothing— a toddler's shoe, a wallet, and a pair of spectacles—lay against the wall like they were just dropped. He stopped and bent down and picked up the glasses. He felt the smooth metal of the frames between his fingers. They haven't made anything like this in probably a hundred years, he thought. He dropped them and continued, putting more speed in his pace.

He halted like the wind was knocked out of him. Sam! He felt her for the first time in months. "Hold on, Sam!" He must be close, he thought. The tunnel took him to a dead end.

He turned around, taking in the rock interior as he paced the small enclosure of rock. He held his hand against the wall. There, another outline in rock. Lucien held his hand over the stone structure until the stalwart material shifted and materialized into an opening. As soon as he put his feet over the entrance, a siren sounded. He knew it couldn't have been that easy.

Lights flashed red throughout this tunnel of steel and copper. "Intruder, an intruder on Level One. "Intruder on Level One." Lucien sprinted through the corridors resembling a military base. He hadn't expected it to be so densely populated. The facility was coated with copper and boron, compromising his abilities. He thought back to his meeting with Zoris and sped to a corner and searched his pockets and hurriedly took the capsule out and went to put it in his mouth. He fumbled, and it dropped and rolled. When he bent to pick it up, a pair of black military boots smashed it in front of him. Lucien's gaze met some heavily armed soldiers pointing high-powered rifles at him.

12 BURNING REALIZATION

Gloria entered the metal doors where she'd left Samantha. They were partway opened. She bent over and picked up the wood board and held it.

"Samantha?" she said out loud.

She gazed at the overturned table and chairs. "Banth."

Would he move her so soon? Had he decided to harvest her eggs, or worse, her soul?

Gloria cringed thinking back in time to her first encounter here. She should have never have gone in the Blue Hole to scuba dive. That was something for the brave, thought Gloria. And scuba diving wasn't something she had planned on doing that night.

* * *

"Gloria, it's like riding a bike," Bobby Nacho said. Of course, that wasn't his real name. Gloria didn't even know what it was.

"Yeah, right," Gloria said shyly.

Gloria put one leg at a time, pulling up the wetsuit, bracing herself on Bobby Nacho's leg. He put the tank on her.

"Open your mouth," he said, holding the regulator against her face.

She took the mouthpiece and put it in her mouth. One by one, they dived into the Blue Hole. Gloria was the next to last to jump.

"Come on, Gloria, you can do it," Bobby Nacho said, cheering Gloria on.

She gave a thumbs-up and took the plunge into the sinkhole.

She swam to the others, deep into the water.

She tried to keep up with her friends, but the water was getting dark, and it was hard to see. She turned and stared up towards the surface, at the nothingness. When she turned around, she couldn't see her friends anymore. She started to panic and tried to resurface. She began to swim in the direction of the surface when she felt something grab her leg. Her legs sprang out, kicking to get free. She broke away and swam as fast as she could to the surface.

Again, something took hold of her leg, then both her legs. Something strong pulled her down, down, down so fast that the scuba gear ripped from her, leaving her to hold her breath on her own. She struggled to hold her breath. Air bubbles escaped Gloria's mouth. She couldn't hold it anymore. The burning realization was upon her. She was drowning. Nothing but blackness until she felt the hard surface hit her body. She lay on the cold, wet cavern of a tunnel until she was thrown on her side.

Something entered her mouth, and a gush of sea water came rushing out. She could breathe. She knew if she played dead, whoever did this would leave. She waited until the only sound was the gurgling of water from the underground stream. Gloria opened her eyes.

She wished she could forget what she saw. Gray, humanlike figures hovered above her.

They tore off her clothes and pulled her into the dark tunnel. She heard an agonizing scream echo. The only voice she recognized was her own.

The one ahead of her was holding her arms, and one behind held her legs. The strange creature laid her down while a man in a military uniform covered her with a blue hospital gown and took her in a shuttle that resembled the kind she'd seen at the New Mexico state fair.

At first, Gloria thought she was at the hospital. She must have almost drowned, and someone saved her, but this was no hospital. She was put on a stretcher, and she was injected with sedatives. She didn't know if it was night or day underground.

She watched, unable to move while two humanoid creatures stood above her.

* * *

Gloria pushed the memories away. She had to figure out where they took Samantha. She feared Samantha had met a worse fate. She too would become a human pincushion like herself. And

Samantha's only hope was for her to find the others and try to convince them to put their attack on hold until Samantha was found.

13 MY ETERNAL DEVOTION

The only place Gloria could think Tarragon and the others might be was at the closed-off section of Dulce. She hadn't traveled down this section since the firefight years ago. Gloria tried to remember how to get there without being seen by any drones. This part of the base was open, with massive cement beams, and shuttles and dump trucks were parked diagonally.

Gloria gazed at the massive fan blowing air through the compound. She noticed medical supplies in plastic canisters and barrels of food. Raul Roman lied, or Banth never told him there was a warehouse full of medical supplies. She came to a heavy metal door half opened. This must be it, she thought. The power was cut off, so she had to pry it open with her hands. She pushed as hard as she could until it opened.

Hanging from the rafters were plastic sheets. She pushed them out of the way until she came to a compartment that was closed off. Dust and charred lab equipment were everywhere. She climbed over the debris. Most of the housing in this area was destroyed in the fire years ago.

Voices were heard coming from the distance. Another door. She pushed hard, almost falling into the crowd of hybrids and her friends.

"Thank God I found you. You have to help!"

"Gloria!" Older ran into her arms. "We thought you were dead."

"Banth would never kill me. He needs me."

"It's almost noon."

"We have to find the human!"

"We have no time to search for someone who made it quite clear she was content to stay in this hell hole."

"No...she's changed her mind. I took her to your housing to be safe. You were gone. I left her to try and find you. It was getting late, so I went back. It was ransacked. It had to be Banth and his soldiers!"

"Little too late? Tarragon said.

"What do I have to do to convince you? You have to help me find Samantha." She knew time was running out. "Soon the tunnels will be filled with Banth's army."

"Now why would I want to help the human?"

She hated how he hated any human. Gloria realized it wasn't his fault. He was the first hybrid human she met on Level Two housing. Level Two was the last stop after genetic testing. Tarragon has never known life outside the secretive underground, and this was the only life he knew existed.

Gloria tried to read Older's expression. He was doing a good job hiding any hint of what he thought.

He was the first human Gloria had met and pretty much the only one she befriended or trusted.

"Older, you have an obligation to save this human. Talk sense into him. You, of all the humans here, know this has gone on too long. Banth plans on moving Samantha to another undisclosed location. I have no idea where, and if he takes her there, she will be lost forever, with no hope of being rescued," Gloria said.

There was a second of silence before anyone spoke again.

"I will help you if he refuses," Older said, brushing shoulders with Tarragon.

"You are much too old, dear friend."

"I'm not that old. I can still fight with the best of them." He winked at Tarragon.

Tarragon gave him a smirk.

"I'm sure you can."

"I can help you, Gloria," Noah said excitedly. Gloria smiled.

"The best and surest way to help is if everyone helps." Gloria locked eyes with Tarragon. He held her gaze.

"What's in it for me?"

"My eternal devotion." She smiled. She knew he couldn't care less about her devotion. A handful of humans and hybrids gathered around them.

"We will help," one said.

Another said, "We all will."

A thin dark-haired woman was the next to speak. "They took the human to the Hallway of Souls. She had an infant with her. Banth has her."

Gloria spun around and faced Tarragon with pleading eyes. "You have to help me. We can't let them take her consciousness. You are the strongest and know Banth's hall better than anyone else."

"Why do you care so much about this human?"

Gloria grimaced at them all but didn't reply.

"Well?"

Older approached Gloria and hugged her.

"Of, of course, we will help, isn't that right, Tarragon?"

Noah stepped forward, then Rek followed and then the other hybrids and humans.

Tarragon gazed at the room before him, not saying anything for a moment, and sighed. He walked towards a beat-up charred rug on the floor and lifted it. Gloria went to where he was. Rek saw what he was doing and aided Tarragon in lifting a compartment under the rug. Gloria's eyes beamed. The secret arsenal was filled with flashguns.

Tarragon held a flashgun high in the air.

"If you were trained in using one of these, step forward," Tarragon shouted. He pulled an old tarp from another floorboard. "If not, take one of Rek's creations. We have frails, blade tomahawk, PVC pipe bow. Whichever you feel comfortable with."

One by one, Tarragon and Rek handed flashguns to the hybrids and humans who gathered in the secret room. Gloria was the first to take a flashgun.

"You sure you know how to use that?" Tarragon said. He bent down and took one along with Older and Noah. The others took what was left. Gloria smiled at Tarragon.

"If we're going to do this, later is not the time. We have to act now."

"Well, let's do it, then," Tarragon said.

They smiled. And off they went out the hidden door of the forgotten hole of Dulce.

Tarragon led the way to the main levels of Dulce. Gloria, Rek, Older, and Noah were at the tail end, followed by twenty or so humans and hybrids. It was almost time for the main lights to be turned on.

Tarragon aimed the flashgun, and one by one, he shot them out. Tarragon knew exactly where he was going—Level Four. They ran through the tunnels, blowing out each drone they came upon. They passed where mind-control experiments were performed on humans. The walls were rocky and curved going through this part of the tunnels.

"Only doctors and scientists are permitted on this level besides top military and Banth," whispered Older.

"This is where the Hallway of Souls and the vats where they grow transgenes beings are."

"I hate this level the most," Gloria said.

They were slow moving through this domain.

She cringed. The huge vats were suspended from the ceiling by a thickly coiled rope. In each cylinder were alien hybrid fetuses growing at each stage of development. Some were almost adult size. A greenish-yellow substance surrounded the fetuses. Gloria knew this was risky, going to the Hallway of Souls, especially because Tarragon and the others had no special abilities.

Gloria scanned the array of botched DNA. Banth and his foot soldiers considered them workers. They were deemed failed gene mutation.

"The cameras at this point were set on timers going on for twenty minutes on and off to conserve energy," Tarragon said in a low voice.

"Best not to shoot them out. If we do, an alarm will sound on this level. We have to bide our time," Rek said in a low voice.

"Agreed," Tarragon replied.

Just when they were about to enter the hallway, a commotion of muffled voices and struggling was heard. Soldiers were yelling, and shots fired.

"Stop," Tarragon said.

He pushed Gloria and the others behind a corner.

Spotlights lit up the tunnel as drones scanned the

area. Soldiers and lab workers were shouting as they wrestled with a man who was soaking wet. They took his arms and legs, carrying him through the tunnel although the man fought and struggled within their grasp. One soldier taped his mouth.

Gloria fixed her eyes on the person. Something about him stirred an emotion she hadn't had in years.

"Is it a human?" Rek asked.

"I can't tell." Tarragon scouted with caution.

"Another helpless soul must have found their way through the hole," Older said, looking at Gloria.

"It seems to be that way," Gloria said softly.

"You appear more than concerned. Almost melancholic, old girl."

She nodded, watching the final soldier go through.

"Tell the others to separate and spread out," Tarragon said.

They crouched back until it was safe to continue to the Hall of Souls.

14 THE BLACK KNIGHT

"Chain the prisoner and prepare a hydrogen drip," Banth said.

He approached Lucien with a smirk across his pasty face. "You do need to cause me anguish, Foster, don't you?" Banth asked Lucien.

"Where is she, Banth?" Lucien said through gritted teeth. He tried to keep calm, but his alien instincts were taking over. He remembered he didn't take the capsule to overshadow the boron and copper coating the dwelling. He tried to shut the lights off with his mind. Nothing. He knew he didn't stand a chance against Banth without his alien abilities. He would be helpless.

Banth stared at Lucien. "Ah hah, Foster, did you forget? I, too, can read minds."

"Shit."

"What are you hiding in your pocket?" Banth said with a sneer.

He patted down Lucien's pockets and took out the remaining capsule and rolled it between his long, gray fingers.

"Let me guess. A magic potion to refract my copper and boron sealant on the compound."

Lucien gritted his teeth.

Lucien watched him take his capsule and place it on the high counter next to the metal table.

"Foster, you can save your strength. You're not special anymore. Your alien powers went bye- bye. The boron is a powerful deflector to your abilities."

Lucien struggled as Banth's guards took him and carried him to the wall. He wrestled with Banth's soldiers, but it didn't do any good. They overtook him. His arms were shackled over his head to the wall.

The taller of the two lab workers hooked up an IV while the other stuck Lucien with a needle. A high-pitched siren sounded.

"Now what?" Banth said. "Leave him and come with me!" Banth yelled. They left through the sliding vacuum door.

Lucien watched the swirling red light on the camera. He struggled with the shackles. He just needed to move the table just enough to get the pill. His legs were free. He lifted his leg and took hold of the table's leg. The pill moved and rolled off the table. Too far. Lucien laughed out loud. If only his hands were free.

The door opened. In came Banth and Dejaha Zoris.

Lucien's brow flexed when he saw Dejaha Zoris. "You tricked me."

Zoris put his hands in his pocket.

"Not exactly." He stood next to Lucien.

"You knew I was coming here." Lucien struggled through the shackles. "Why?"

Dejaha Zoris lowered his chin and opened his mouth to speak when Banth stopped him.

"Because of you. You need to know the truth," Banth chimed in.

"What are you talking about? What truth?" Lucien's jaw clenched. Banth and Dejaha Zoris were quiet a moment.

"Your birthright," Banth said. His lip curled into a twisted smile, showing his jagged teeth.

"Just let me take Samantha back to the ranch. She can't help you." Lucien knew he had to get free, or at least get them to let him go.

"Foster, we need you, and we need the girl," Banth said. He pulled up a chair. "Zoris, do you want to tell him, or should I?"

Zoris's attention went to Lucien.

"Tell me what?" Lucien yelled, pulling at the shackles.

"The Black Knight," said Zoris.

Lucien's eyes scanned the two.

"Yes. The Black Knight is en route for Earth again." Banth smiled and took a breath. "The satellite that has been orbiting the Earth for centuries," Banth said.

Lucien's head was spinning, trying to grasp the meaning of this conversation.

"The phantom satellite?" Lucien said, his eyes rocketing between the two of them.

"Yes...the said satellite. The Oracle. The receiver to the supreme beacon. He doesn't remember."

"The Black Knight is a beacon to what?" Lucien said.

"To the Kingdom of the Serpent," Banth said. He smiled.

"Zoris doesn't seem to think it's humorous," Lucien said, studying Zoris's expression. "I have no idea what you're talking about."

"You are one of us, Foster, just as I am and so is Zoris. But you are special."

Banth stood and walked up to Lucien, glaring at him straight in the eye. "At least not in a sense the humans you think we are."

"What are you talking about?" Lucien said. Beads of sweat began to form on his brow.

"Lucien, I am afraid to be the one to tell you. Yes, you are—"

"Not from Moira, not a planet but an interdimensional palace. Where the light himself threw his finest," Zoris interrupted.

"You're both mad!" Lucien spat out as he struggled with the chains. "If I am so special—if what you say is true—why do you want Sam? Leave her out of it. I am what you really want."

"Because we need her. She's special. Her blood mixed. She did not die. She's the chosen one. We could never conceive a child with such splendid blood. We need her. You need her. She will be your queen and conquer the light." He laughed."

"You're insane!"

"We will leave you to your thoughts on your newfound legacy."

"What thoughts! There's nothing to think about. There is no legacy."

Banth left through the sliding door.

Dejaha Zoris lingered a moment and glanced back at Lucien as if to say something and changed his mind. He left as well.

As soon as the two were gone, Lucien struggled with the chains and searched the ground for the pill that Michael gave him. There it was, right near his black leather boot.

15 SHE'S JUST ONE HUMAN

Tarragon held Gloria back cautiously. They rounded the corner until they reached the Hall of Souls. He led his armed party of thirty or so through the ominous underpass until he came the entryway to the walls of strung skeletons and Removers' domain. He motioned for the others to wait at the entrance. The darkness was illuminated with a blue light. A glass case held the consciousness of the souls of the innocent humans whose bodies were replaced with the foot soldiers of Dulce. Each case radiated a bright aura of a soul—pink, red, blue, purple—and some were even black. Gloria followed Tarragon in. No one spoke, giving the scene an even creepier ambiance.

Gloria slowly went to each case and stood. The spectrum of different colors shone on her face as she made her way, stopping at each case and gliding her hand across the smooth glass. Tarragon and Older followed.

"This is the work of pure evil."

"What makes you think they took her here?" Tarragon asked Gloria. He peered over his shoulder, gripping his weapon.

"It doesn't look like she's here. Unless it's already been done," Rek said.

"You'd never be able to tell which one is hers anyway." Tarragon went by the entry. "I don't like it here."

"He just wants her DNA. I overheard him. Maybe she's not here after all," Gloria said, searching the cases.

"Where does he have her, then?"

"This is good she's not here. We have to keep searching."

"No, we don't. I said I would take you here. This is as far as we are going. The Revolt. We have to act now," Tarragon said.

"But—" Gloria tried to reason with him.

"I have to agree with Tarragon this time, old friend," Older said.

"He's right, it's now or never," Rek said.

"Now!" Someone from Tarragon's army yelled.

"Gloria, Tarragon is right. We must think about the rebellion. If we wait, Banth's foot soldiers will be awakened," Older said, comforting Gloria.

"She's just one human."

Gloria was outnumbered. They all agreed with Tarragon that it wasn't safe for them here.

Gloria knew he spoke the truth. They'd come

this far, what was a few more minutes? They left the Hall of Souls. She felt defeated and angry she couldn't convince Tarragon and the others into searching more.

The group split up. Noah and the others headed through a warren that was close to Level One communications room. Gloria, Tarragon, Rek, and Older went to Level Four.

They were just about to cross over onto Level Four when they heard laughter. It was Banth and someone that Gloria had only seen a few times. The two laughed between themselves, coming out of one of the interrogation rooms. They rounded the hallway. Their snickers echoed.

Older held Gloria's arm. They watched them disappear in the distance. They all took a breath. Gloria sighed to calm down.

"They must have someone very special in there," Rek said.

"The human?" Older answered dryly.

Gloria started to approach the door.

"What do you think you're doing?" Tarragon said, stopping her. Gloria didn't want to answer. She yanked her arm away from his grip.

"Maybe it's Samantha!"

Tarragon shook his head.

"We have to see." She would go herself, but she knew if there were guards inside, she would be defenseless. She wasn't going ask for Tarragon's assistance.

"...and then you're on your own."

Gloria nodded.

Tarragon held the flashgun, pointing at the door. This was the only room that didn't have a glass window. Tarragon pushed the door open.

"It's not locked," Gloria said, surprised.

"Banth's sure confident that no one was going to enter," Older said. They stopped abruptly.

Gloria looked at the wall with chains hoping it was Samantha.

"It's one of the Fosters," Older said.

"You—" Gloria said as she hurried to his side.

"How do you know my name!" Lucien said, pulling on the chains.

"You shouldn't be here."

The room became quiet.

Gloria saw the pill near his boot. She picked it up.

"I don't know who you are. But I need that."

Gloria glanced down at the pill.

Tarragon snatched it from her.

"What is it?" she said, taking it from Tarragon's hand.

"It doesn't concern you," said Lucien.

"Some sort of elixir," Tarragon said. Rek approached.

"Yes, this permits you to use your alien gifts, doesn't it?" Rek said, smiling at Lucien.

"Yes, give it to me! Put it in my mouth. I have to find her."

"Samantha! So, you're the one she's talked about," Gloria said.

"You saw her!" Lucien said with a furrowed brow. "You have to give me the pill!"

"And if we help you?" Tarragon said sharply.

"I can help you! All of you!" Lucien pulled at his chains. "With my help, you can leave this place."

"Give him the pill," Tarragon said.

Gloria put the pill in Lucien Foster's mouth, and they waited for it to take effect. Lucien lifted his arms, and the chains broke. The shackles fell from his ankles. Like magic, he was free.

"Tell me where Sam is," Lucien said persistently.

"She can be in any one of the tunnels," Gloria said with a grimace.

"Banth took her somewhere," Older said.

Lucien opened the door and paused.

"You're going to leave here and do what? You just can't barge out demanding the human," Tarragon said, throwing his weight at Lucien, towering over him like an elk over a possum.

"And what? You going to stop me?"

Tarragon didn't need to speak. Older did for him.

"You have no idea what rabbit hole you fell into, do you?" Older said harshly at Lucien.

"What is this rabbit hole you speak of?" Rek

said.

Older ignored the hybrid.

"And you're not going to ruin the rebellion," Tarragon finished.

"You're not the brightest crayon in the box, are you?" Lucien said.

"You two speak in riddles," Rek said. He looked at Older. "What's this crayon?"

"I wouldn't think too hard about it, ole boy. Maybe if we get out of here, I will buy you a box," Older said with a smile.

The air was thick, and Gloria knew Tarragon and Older were right.

"Tarragon, Lucien isn't going to start something he can't finish. Lucien, isn't that right?" Gloria urged.

Lucien nodded patiently.

Older stepped forward between Tarragon and Lucien.

"What Tarragon is trying to say...We don't know where Samantha is, and if we did, the underground dwellers of Dulce will be waking. And when that happens, every tunnel will be filled with Banth's foot soldiers," Older said.

Lucien was quiet as he listened.

"Samantha..."

Gloria didn't know how to address her condition. "Dulce is a lab for genetic engineering. Samantha was injured."

"I'm aware. She was shot in West Virginia,"

Lucien said.

"She was shot multiple times. And Banth performed tests." Gloria hesitated a moment. "She's weak from the tests."

"Tests...what kind of tests?"

"Medical tests." She was quiet for a moment. "A bone marrow extraction." Gloria's voice faded.

Gloria waited for him to take in what she said. She wasn't sure if she should have told him.

"What do they want with her marrow?"

"I don't know," she said.

Gloria knew why Banth wanted her bone marrow. She just wasn't going to tell this stranger.

Gloria inched close to Lucien. "Samantha's life is in grave danger, and if you leave this room, the Watchers, or worse, the Fallen, will find you."

"Or the Removers," Rek added.

"Your unique talents are no match for theirs," Older said. "You have a better chance putting those shackles on and waiting for Banth to return and take him out then."

"Or we all leave together," Gloria said.

16 COUNT ORLOK

I found myself surrounded by elegant furnishings. I rubbed my deceiving eyes. "This is one of your tricks, isn't it?"

"It's real."

"Where am I?"

"The upper location of Dulce," Banth said.

I gazed at the walls painted in white, an oak bookcase, a beige leather couch and loveseat, a crystal chandelier, and light-colored hardwood flooring with a flowered throw rug with pastels. I could smell Toll House cookies like my mom used to make.

"What is this place?"

"Whatever I desire," Banth said with a crooked smile.

I wasn't quite sure how I ended up here—another one of Banth's mind tricks for sure. I should know better than to be caught off guard.

All at once, I was dressed in a fitted red silk evening gown. Red carpet perfect for sure. I went to stand in front of a vast crystal mirror above a wet bar.

I had to do a double take because the reflection resembled nothing like I remembered. My hair was the exact color of Lucien's; my eyes didn't look like zombie eyes any longer. It was like I was gazing into Lucien's. They had the same snowy white diamond glitter to them.

My hair cascaded down past my shoulders, and smooth, framing my face. My neck was adorned with a diamond petal pendant and matching earrings. I took in a deep breath. I wasn't sure if I was dreaming or imagining this.

"It is real, Samantha," Banth said, reading my mind and facing me all at once. He stood back with his hand on his chin, admiring his creation. "Do you approve of my taste in female attire?"

"What is this all for? And why am I here and where is here?" I said, bracing myself for some sort of devious plan on Banth's part.

He walked over to me, almost gliding in a strange paranormal way like the 1922 German vampire movie Nosferatu. For some reason, I stayed put just watching him.

"You hurt my feelings. I think I am much more attractive than Count Orlok."

I could feel the hair on my neck stand on end. Being in the same room so close made my heart quicken.

"How is any of this possible?"

"So many questions." He smiled in his creepy

way. "I will get to them in a moment, but first I have a proposition for you."

Here it comes. He smiled, most likely reading my mind again.

"How would you like to live here with me? With all the luxuries you could ever want."

Was he out of his mind? With him?

"Like some twisted Beauty and the Beast movie!"

"You would never have to do without–jewels, anything you want."

"You really think I want jewels?"

I grimaced at the thought of staying here underground with him.

"Isn't that what most humans want? An abundance of material goods?"

"No..."

"Anything you desire, I would provide." He stepped closer.

I flinched.

"Stay underground in this rat hole with you? No! I want to go back home to my father." I started for the door. But there wasn't one.

"Samantha, where are you going? Don't you want to stay with the baby! Your baby–"

I stopped and turned.

"What did you say?" I said, walking in his direction. My heart was beating wildly deep within my chest.

"Your baby."

I took a deep breath. My head spun. Did I hear him right?

"You're lying."

"I would never lie about that."

"For real. Whose baby is it?"

"Yours and Mr. Foster's."

I felt my knees buckle and the room began to spin. I didn't feel the ground until my head hit it hard.

* * *

I felt something wet on my face. I opened my eyes, and it was Ruby.

"I missed you, I missed you." My new four-legged friend jumped up on the bed I was lying on and licked my face. Her ruby eyes glowed. "Oh girl, how did you get here?"

Ruby rolled until she was lying on her back with her feet in the air. "You want a belly rub, don't you?" I rubbed her belly until she turned around, snuggling her nose into my neck. I petted and kissed her. "I must have passed out Ruby."

I sat up in a lavish bed with an antique carved headboard and sleigh bed footboard. The bedspread was made of silk and pink ribbon.

I didn't know for sure where I was. This was nothing like Dulce. A canopy bassinet covered in ivory lace with gold trim was at the foot of the bed. I inched my way off the bed. Ruby jumped down and went to sit in front of the bassinet.

"What do you think, Ruby? Is Banth telling the truth?" Ruby barked.

"Is he really mine?"

Ruby barked again.

"My baby."

Was it true? The baby sleeping soundly in the bassinet was my baby, Lucien's and mine. I felt my body begin to tremble as I stood slowly and walked to the bassinet. There he was sleeping. My baby with pink skin. I touched his little hand, so soft like nothing I ever felt.

Ruby sat down next to me, cocking her head. I wondered if I should listen to Banth and just be content taking care of this small part of Lucien and myself. And then doubt swooped in like a jet plane. What if this wasn't our baby? What if this was an experiment that was done to me? I didn't trust my own thoughts. I tried to calculate when I left with Lucien in the sky and when I was brought back.

I heard footsteps, and then the French doors opened behind me.

"Go ahead and pick him up. No one is here to take him from you. No Removers or Watchers. You are safe. I promise." I listened to his voice without turning around. Like in a trance, I scooped the infant into my arms, bringing his tiny head to my nose. I smelled him, taking in his sweet scent.

Banth spoke in a clear and precise tone.

"The child is yours. You have my word," he said

quietly, maybe not to disturb the sleeping baby in my arms. I turned.

"How can that be? It hasn't been that long." It takes nine months of gestation for a baby to be formed.

"Yes, a human baby, Samantha. It does."

"A human baby," I echoed his words.

"His father is not human, and either are you anymore."

He approached me. His sickly features didn't scare me anymore. I guess it made me different now. I was no longer human. Just like the shepherd watching me. I was like her, a mixture of alien DNA.

"You are changing at a remarkable rate. Doesn't surprise me. You are the chosen one. We have been waiting for you for centuries."

"I am not your chosen one, Banth."

I put the infant without a name down and walked through the French doors, hoping he would follow and not disturb the sleeping baby. Ruby was right at my heels. Banth followed, closing the doors. I watched him pour himself a drink of brandy, putting his long, gray finger in the glass and stirring the golden liquid.

I felt my stomach turn as I looked away.

"May I pour you one?"

"No."

"Suit yourself, my dear. Or would you prefer something else, maybe a chocolate chip cookie and some milk— perhaps a Dr. Pepper? I know all your likes and dislikes Samantha Hunter?"

I laughed out loud. "You know, if this were any other place in the world, that would be tempting. But here right now with you sounds like one of my worst nightmares! You are a disgusting, vile **SOB**, and I'd rather die a hundred deaths than end up here in this make-believe world you created. Do I make myself perfectly clear!" I was not sure where the words came from as they shot from my mouth.

"I like a girl who speaks from her heart."

"You don't even have a heart."

"Actually, I have a beautiful twelve-chamber heart."

"I want to leave this place, and I want to go now." I peered over to the door, but it was nowhere. I tried to piece together how I got here. "Where are my clothes I had on?" I paced the hardwood floors. Banth didn't answer right away. He watched.

"Those rags?"

"I'd rather die underground than stay here another minute with you," I said through gritted teeth. "Don't you get it?"

I started to remove the jewels from my body and ripped the barrette from my hair.

"Do you know what you are, Samantha Hunter?" Banth said. "You are more than an oracle to house a new species. You are the queen bee, my dear. We extracted all your eggs from your womb."

His words cut like a knife.

"You did what—" I pounced at him.

He began to laugh at my effort to hurt him. He pushed me off him and laughed some more. "We've already begun the process." I held my hand over my belly.

"You evil, despicable monster."

"What is... evil? Without good. Bingo! You win!"

"You had no right."

"Oh, but I did."

I just stared at his repulsive face.

"You haven't a clue."

"But I'm sure you'll tell me."

"Soon your DNA and future generations will populate this planet. It is only a matter of time before we terminate every human left on Earth. The virus is already in action." He sat down, happy with his words.

"Your virus to destroy humanity?" I thought back to Oakridge Estates and the news bulletin. So, this was their plan to annihilate the human population and replace it with their DNA, using me as their vessel to repopulate.

"Exactly."

"How many are dead?" I asked, thinking of my father. "How many, Banth?" His answer was quick.

"At least half, as I recall."

Everything was moving fast. The walls felt like they were caving in around me. I couldn't breathe.

"My father?"

He seemed almost sad.

"He is alive for the time being."

At least that I knew. If I was no longer human and more alien. Why couldn't I read his mind?

Banth smiled. "Because you will never be fully like Foster, my dear. Your children will be my hybrids but a very beautiful hybrid, not like myself or the other creatures of the underworld. You have a lot to learn about who we are. Just like the night, there is darkness you can't see. Just the wars that you can see. But you will see and understand in time. You don't have a choice. You can't leave here. You are safe underground. I am offering you the chance to stay here and be a mother to this child. Your offspring, yours and Lucien Foster's."

"It's true? That baby is our child together? But how? I don't understand."

"Does it really matter? It won't change anything."

"Did you take my eggs and combine them with Lucien's..."

He smiled. "No, Samantha, we harvested your eggs after your baby was conceived. When you were on the Black Knight. We let nature take its course."

"*The Black Knight?*"

"The Oracle. The vessel to the abyss."

I grimaced. *Why can't I remember such a memorable event with someone I love deeply?*

"Because what fun is that?" Banth grinned.

"Stop reading my mind!" I raised my hand, and he went flying into the wall. I raised my other hand, lifting a vase. "I guess I have just enough alien DNA in me to do that!"

Banth lay shaking on the ground, laughing. "Good job, Samantha, dear! Why don't you relax and lower the vase? And I will give you your memory back."

"Is this another one of your despicable tricks?"

He smiled and shook his head. "You have my word."

"And that means nothing to me!"

I lowered the vase. Banth slowly stood, fixing his black slacks and jacket. "I will give you your pathetic memory of your union with the Foster boy. And of the baby."

"So, help me God, if this is a trick, there will be hell to pay."

"God the father, or God the son, oh, wait, let me guess, the Holy Spirit."

"Stop mocking me!"

"It just dawned on me...aren't you from the town of Trinity? How ironic is that, don't you think?"

"I think you better stop while you're ahead."

"Now, now, simmer down and get comfy. Lie down on the sofa and close your eyes. I will leave you to your thoughts."

"Tell me the truth, is this a trick?"

"Unfortunately for you, it's the truth."

I followed Banth's instructions, and as soon as he departed, I lay down with Ruby at my side. I closed my eyes and waited for my memories to come back. I soon fell into a deep slumber.

17 AURORA'S CURTAIN

The air was cold and the light bright, as bright as midafternoon sun. I didn't need to see where I was; all I had to do was think, and I knew what was in front of me. But I didn't know exactly where here was, but I knew it was not a place I should be. I should have listened to Lucien and not taken hold of him. I heard unfamiliar voices speaking, but I could not understand. Then all I saw were Lucien's eyes.

His eyes were my guide through the mist, lighting the way through the storm. He took my hand, and I wasn't afraid anymore. He spoke through his mind without words, and I could understand him. He took my hand and told me to follow him, and I did.

"Sam, why didn't you stay with Cassiel?"

I didn't answer.

I scanned the area. We were inside a vast ray of shimmering pink and green light in space, twirling through the stars. "Where is this place?" I said without fear.

"We are in the middle of an Aurora Borealis's curtain of light."

"A curtain to heaven," I said.

Low on the horizon, I noticed a faint luminosity of jade color light that formed an arch, stretching lazily across the sky. As time passed, bands of light formed and drifted above, slowly brightening to form giant curtains in the heavens that slowly waved as if a gentle wind were blowing. Suddenly, the bottom of the curtains brightened with a pinkish tint and rippled fast. Azure and purple colors appeared. As the curtains passed directly overhead, I saw bright points of light that swirled like a sparkler on the Fourth of July. The entire sky seemed to be full of color and motion. Then, after several minutes, everything faded into a warm green glow.

"Are we alone?"

"In this matrix, we are."

"How is any of this possible? Is this an altered reality?"

"Just take my hand, so we don't separate."

"Where are we going?"

"I'm not sure where we are?"

Everything changed into a beautiful forest with lush green trees, and velvet green moss under my feet. Lucien was dressed as he always was. I was barefoot and wearing a short skirt and summer blouse, and we were laughing.

"Lucien, are we home?"

"No," he said, laughing.

I stepped forward onto the green moss.

"It's so soft. Oh, my God, I've never felt anything so soft."

"Stay close."

"Is this heaven?"

"You'd think."

"Are we dead?"

"We are in another dimension."

I started to laugh.

I opened my hands and inspected my palms. I could see through them. "This is incredible," I said.

He held my hand and kissed me full on the lips. I kissed him back. Slowly, he unbuttoned my blouse. I wasn't at all shy. I had no inhibitions as my blouse fell to the ground. I smiled, as did he. He picked me up. I wrapped my legs around his torso.

"I feel so different. I can't explain it. Like I have cravings."

"Like an incredible appetite. I know."

"I'm so hungry." I laughed.

He kissed me again. This time longer. "I want you," he said.

"I feel so alive here."

"Like nothing else matters but you and me."

It was as if he breathed me back to life with each kiss. I felt him like I had never felt him before.

He bent down, his lips against my cheek, brushing it lightly—and still, that delicate touch sent shivers through my nerves, shivers that made my whole body tremble.

We were moving in slow motion, but we weren't. He laid me down softly on the moss. It felt like air against my back. He lay on top me. His lips felt like velvet on my skin.

"If you want me to stop, tell me now," he whispered. When I didn't say anything, he brushed his mouth against the hollow of my temple. My head tilted back, staring up at the mystical sky.

"I don't."

He kissed me again.

He traced the line of my cheekbone.

"Or now." His lips were on mine. "Or—"

"No. I never want you to stop."

I reached up and pulled him down to me, and the rest of his words were lost against my mouth. He kissed me gently, carefully, like he knew every inch of me. But it wasn't gentleness I wanted, not now, not after all this time in space. I knotted my fists in his shirt, pulling him hard against me.

He groaned softly, low in his throat, and then his arms circled me, gathering me against him, and we rolled over on the grass, tangled together, kissing in this enchanted world far away from anyone. Like a dream come true.

Then came the most beautiful moment of my whole life passing in seconds before me. I stopped and gazed into his eyes as if my mind was taking a snapshot to savor this moment in time forever.

He kissed me on the lips. The whole world

might have turned upside down, then left me behind. Lost in this forbidden, magical Aurora's curtain where time and space coexisted somewhere light years away from Earth. There I was alone with Lucien. And I felt I had been given a gift, and told just to keep it, not to look at it—a star in the sky, infinitely precious, wrapped up with silver and gold, the radiant light seared through, the revelation blissful, more powerful than a religious experience!

Finally, we were one. Our bodies moved in rhythm together. At that moment, I knew we were creating something beautiful. I knew we were no longer just two souls but three.

Time moved in rhythm with our souls. How could this be? Time was moving fast but slow. I heard a small heartbeat. I laughed. Then I felt my belly move. And then it began to grow inside me.

What was happening in this strange place? I could almost hear celestial music. We were moving fast through the stars. Then everything changed again. We were walking through a busy three-dimensional city. People resembled us, but their eyes all glowed the same snowy ice as Lucien's. We were living here together but apart.

We were happy. Yes, happy in our new life. Life was good.

Like a montage in a movie, all at once I was in a white-washed kitchen tossing a fresh green salad with unusual vegetables I had never seen before. I could see Lucien tending a garden. I peered in the distance from our castle along a seashore. I paused a moment to watch Lucien kneel in the sandy garden, tending to exotic fruits and vegetables. He was barefoot, wearing white slacks and a white short-sleeve shirt. A gentle breeze blew open sheer white curtains. I was chopping veggies of some kind. I took one and bit into a savory flower. A multitude of flavors danced on my tongue. I never tasted anything so sweet before. I was happy watching Lucien.

I bent down to examine my swollen belly. I held my hand over it and felt life under my fingertips and smiled. For the first time in my life, I was truly blissful with happiness.

Lucien caught sight of me watching and smiled. He took off his gardening gloves and set them down and joined me. He took one of the veggies I was eating and bit it.

He brushed a strand of hair from my cheek. "You look radiant."

"You're just saying that because it's true." I laughed.

I took the vegetable, which resembled a carrot, that was hanging out his mouth and bit it. "I never thought I could be this happy. I wish it would never end."

"Who says it has to end?"

"Seriously, we can't stay here forever, Lucien."

"Why not?"

"Because none of it's real."

 I felt a pain in my belly, taking me by surprise.

"That sure felt real."

"What is it?"

"I don't know.

"Sam!"

I felt a gush of wetness between my thighs. "I think my water just broke."

Lucien studied the ground, looking at the puddle of pink liquid. "I think you're right."

"It's only been—"

"Why does that surprise you?" He laughed.

I felt another twinge of pain. "It's time." A nervous laugh sprang from my lips.

"Let's go!" Lucien took me in his arms.

"Oh my God! This is really happening!"

I patted my belly. "Okay, little baby, it's time to meet your mommy and daddy."

He took my hand, and with a thought, we were walking into a tall glass building. People came and went. We checked in to what resembled like a hospital reception area.

"Lucien Foster and Samantha Hunter. Wellness is expecting us."

A woman wearing a face mask helped me to a wheelchair. Lucien was right at my side. They wheeled me into a strange room with blue lighting and waterfall walls. Two more masked people came in dressed all in white. Lucien tried to comfort me, but they wouldn't let him stay.

They removed my clothes and draped me in some type of plastic sheet. It covered me from the neck down. I was terrified of what was happening. My belly protruded, although covered.

A man wearing a blue mask took my legs. "She is completely dilated," he said through the mask. The lighting seemed to dim except for a blue beam of light coming from all sides of the room. Another person came in and settled next to the man.

"He's asking to see her. Should I let him in?"

"It's fine."

Lucien came rushing in the sliding door. A beam of blue light bounced off his gray eyes. He smiled with worry and took my hand in his and squeezed it tight.

I could feel beads of sweat forming on my brow. "You're going to be a mom," he said while smiling.

"I'm scared."

"This is a piece of cake."

"It hurts bad, Lucien."

"The wellness officers are in control. At the right moment, they will ease the baby from your womb." I watched through the mirror above us. Lucien was right.

A misty cloud came from a fixture from the ceiling. All at once, the pain left. In its place came joy and bliss.

"Okay, Samantha... on the count of two, I want

you to give me a big push. Once you do it, you will feel a slight pinch and then your baby will be born."

"Just a pinch? You sure?"

Lucien took my hand.

Just like the wellness officer said, I pushed. When I did, an AI android scooped in and removed the baby with his artificial hands. It was so different from a birth on Earth. There was no blood, no screaming, and pain. The plastic draping covering my body pulled back from my breasts. The baby was placed just above my belly. A calmness swept over when a white mist was rereleased from the ceiling fan. The wellness officer latched the baby's mouth to my breast, and it began to nurse.

"It will help you relax," the wellness officer said.

Lucien took the baby's finger in his. The baby's tiny finger closed around his.

"This is so surreal," I said with tears in my eyes.

"I love you, Samantha."

"Our baby is perfect."

"Yes, it is," a voice coming in from the sliding door said. We both looked up. Although the person was wearing a surgical mask I could tell by the eyes it was a woman.

"We weren't expecting you so soon," the male wellness officer said.

"I was invited."

Lucien stood. "By whom?"

"It was only a matter of time." The woman

wellness officer said.

"It's a male, as we were expecting," the other wellness officer said, taking the baby from my chest.

"No. They can't do this," I said.

"Oh, but we can."

* * *

Just like it never happened, I was back on the sofa.

I opened my eyes and sat up hating Banth more than ever. I pondered upon what I'd seen thoroughly.

How could they take this memory away from me? How cruel. Banth was telling the truth. My child wasn't made in a lab? But this didn't make sense. When I returned, why didn't the doctor see that I had just given birth?

The door burst open.

"Your birth was not like a human birth; the wellness officers made sure of that. Your human doctors had no idea. After you gave birth, Dr. O'Neil took it."

"I knew I recognized those olive eyes."

"She tried to deceive me and kept the baby from me for a time." She wasted my time at Oakridge Estates when all along she had the baby and knew where the Foster boy was. She'd have me drug you for nothing with the possibility of damaging your precious DNA gems. She finally wised up and realized she needed me. Your Foster boy was kept in limbo for a while in the Aurora's Curtain. That's all you need to know for now."

"I had a baby?"

"Yes, you did."

"You evil, sick monster. You took it."

"And the rest of your eggs are in a safe place."

"It's really mine! My baby."

"And your baby. Aww, memories. Hallmark moments. Yes?"

"I don't believe you. That baby in there is not mine. That's a newborn. If it were mine, it would be almost a year old."

"Your baby developed faster than the normal human pregnancy on the Black Knight. Once we got back to Earth, we needed to slow down the rate of its growth to prevent gene mutation. We needed to monitor its growth. Like your Lucien, who is well into 70 Earth years. But in otherworldly years, once development has gotten to the perfect age, the aging process halts. So basically, he robbed the cradle with you. Sorry to be the one to tell, but yes, that baby lying in the bassinet in the other room is yours."

"I don't want it. Keep it." I couldn't believe my own ears.

"But it's your flesh and blood, my dear. Surely you don't want one of the government's nannies or one of the hybrids here to care for it. Do you?"

I felt the sting of a tear rolling down my check.

"Why didn't you just kill me? Why did you bring

me back?" I said, wishing again this was a nightmare.

"Because your baby has a rare blood disease. A severe form of it. Aplastic anemia that must run in your bloodline, maybe not the wisest choice when creating a new life, but you lived when Mr. Foster gave you the blood transfusion. The aplastic anemia can be overlooked; it's treated with a stem cell transplant. That is what we did."

"So, it's not perfect like you wanted. You have no use for it."

"Oh, but we do have a use for it. We can correct that with genetic engineering. You saw firsthand what most of the hybrids look like. None look as perfect as the baby in the next room."

"I saw the other babies. They look normal."

"Oh, but they aren't. They are useless. None have any abilities like your baby will have. Come." Banth opened the French doors.

The baby was lying in the bassinet awake, looking up, its legs and arms moving.

Banth took a bottle and held it in his hands, standing above the baby. The baby made a cooing sound. "Watch."

The bottle lifted from Banth's hand and went right to the baby's mouth. Banth smiled.

I watched the baby drink from the bottle in amazement.

"To more pressing matters, are you going to stay with me as my bride?"

I didn't answer him.

All I could think of was my baby in the bassinet suckling his bottle.

"Make your decision before I change my mind." Banth left me to my thoughts.

What was I going to do? I had to escape this place and find Gloria.

I searched the suite for something to put on instead of this gown. My mind drifted back to Halloween last year. And that stupid costume. Remembering seemed so surreal. I wanted to go back. I wanted to try and redo that night when Lucien told me who he was. I played that moment over in my mind when he told me he was an alien. Why didn't I keep running? I should have never stopped. I rushed to the other room and began searching that room. I suddenly thought of Finn. I heard a cough.

"Finally! Where the heck have you been?" I said.

Ruby saw him too. "How can she see you?" I said, watching Ruby run in circles and lick him.

"Not sure."

"She's bonded with you. Maybe she's imprinted on you."

Finn chuckled while petting the alien pup. "Why are you wearing an evening gown? Going somewhere?"

"Banth is a crazy psycho alien mutant. He has some ludicrous idea about keeping me here with him to raise my baby."

I ran to the French door to the bedroom where the bassinet was. I looked down at the bassinet with tears in my eyes. Finn followed me. I reached in and took the bottle and picked up the baby, cradling it. "How could this have happened?" Tears were now streaking down my cheeks when the door flung open. It was Banth and his military guards.

"Take the baby," he shouted.

"No!" I screamed, holding the baby tight.

A guard pulled the now crying baby from my arms.

"Banth! Why are you doing this? You said you would give me time to think!"

Finn vanished.

The guard handed my baby over to Banth. The room filled with Banth's guards and men in suits surrounded the place.

The baby began to wail.

"Wait, wait. I'll stay, damn you. I'll stay!"

"It's too late. I was going to let you stay here until Foster decided to rescue his damsel in distress."

"Lucien's here?" I struggled to free myself from his guards. "Where is he?" I screamed.

"You're wasting your breath, Samantha," I heard a voice say from the outer room.

Four men in suits wearing earpieces stood firm. The Secret Service? I couldn't believe my eyes.

"Where is it?" a tall man wearing a dark blue suit

and a red tie and a flag pin on his lapel said.

"You're in on this!" I recognized him right away. It was the President of the United States. He stopped in front of Banth. The Secret Service men were right at his side.

"Where is it, Banth?"

"Here, take it," he said, hardly looking at me. "Aren't you going to ask if it's a boy or girl?" Banth said with a snicker.

"Why?" I asked the President.

The president scowled at me. "Once the virus annihilates every human alive, we will need to repopulate Earth. This infant will be the beginning."

"You're one of them?" Disbelief set in.

"I am."

I wasn't going to let them do this. I mustered all the strength I had. I could feel my eyes begin to get hot. I concentrated as hard as I could. I didn't even have to lift a finger. Ruby felt it too because her hair began to rise on her back. And all at once, she was full grown, showing her teeth with a growl. She snarled, showing white fangs. Her hair stood on end.

"What is this?" the president said. Banth backed away.

"Let my baby go!" I said through gritted teeth. I pulled away from the guards.

"How's this possible? I thought she wouldn't have any powers," the president said to Banth.

"Lower the copper," Banth yelled.

The ceiling beams retracted, and copper panels were lowered. I could feel the surge of electricity that was powering my special gifts leave my body. I was once again the human I once was.

I watched the president and Banth and their guards leave me. As soon as they left, the room suddenly changed like magic. The beautiful crystal chandelier, the hardwood flooring, cathedral ceiling, the white roman pillars and French doors transformed into what they were all along, a gray cell surrounded by glass. It was all some sort of optical illusion mind trick.

"I have to find a way out of here," I said out loud. "I can't let them take my baby and dissect him and use him to make their super alien/human hybrid." Then it hit me. I felt defeated.

"Cassiel!"

I thought if I screamed his name, he would somehow hear me.

"Finn." I looked up at the copper panels still visible. They must have been in all the cells. I didn't see any in the tunnels. Yes, there wouldn't be. How could the Removers and Watchers do their bidding for Banth?

I wished I had eaten the slop they brought me. At least I would have some energy to get out of this mess. I was famished. I was in the corner, resting my head on my knees when the sliding door opened. It was Raul Roman and Agent Harmon and two other guards.

"You!" He tried to kill all the hybrids at the underground bunker at the Greenbrier hotel. "You hate human and alien hybrids. You almost blew them up."

"Samantha, you should have died at Greenbrier. Now you are going to." I looked at Raul Roman. "Banth thinks you're working for him. He'll find out and kill you."

"I'd sooner die than let him succeed in his plan."

"You're an Illuminati too?"

"Take the prisoner," Raul Roman said. The two guards grabbed my arms. I struggled. "Take me where?" I yelled. "Where are you taking me?"

I kicked and wiggled within the guard's grip.

"Banth and the president have come to a decision. They will make more hybrids with your DNA. We are not going to let that happen," Raul Roman said and paused. "And unfortunately for you- you are not included in their plans."

"You're going to kill me?"

"And all the babies and embryos will be destroyed," Harmon said.

"Noooo! My baby! What have they done with my baby!"

"You should have gone along with his bizarre plans for you," Raul Roman said. "At least you would have been safe."

"You aren't like them. I saw it in your eyes."

"You saw nothing," Raul Roman said.

"You're not going to kill me?"

"You're right. What's going to happen to you is worse than death," Agent Harmon said.

The guard held a flashgun and pointed at me and fired.

I was paralyzed. The guard lifted me over his shoulders. I could see but could not move my limbs. My sight was distorted, seeing everything upside down. He stopped and dumped me against a wall and took my arms and shackled them to a pole. He turned and left the same way he came.

* * *

The room was dark except for glowing lights of different colors in glass cylinders. Red, blue, green, and yellow pulsated. Hanging from vats were human bodies suspended with tubes breathing for them. Gloria told me about this place! The Hall of Souls.

I lay there, not being able to move. I watched Raul Roman and Harmon talk among themselves and then leave.

Little by little, the feeling came back to my hands and feet. I pulled at the shackles and stood. "Lucien! I need you! Gloria!" I screamed and pulled.

The room became bright, blinding me. Black feathers blew in the air, and the smell of sulfur filled my lungs. Out of the corner of the room, a creature slivered in front of me. It moved, almost gliding, in my direction. It had delicate features, making me think it was female. Its face looked human with dark hollow eyes and its skin as white as snow. Matted, disheveled silver hair hung from its scalp to below its shoulders. When it breathed, charcoal wings moved in out from its body like an accordion. A burlap garment draped its hairless body, leaving the wings exposed.

"We use the blood and body parts of humans as a formula. Food...you might say—it's what keeps them alive. Like mother's milk. It's in the vats you see. They're artificial wombs. Like the one inside you. I heard Banth took what was yours away. Those tiny pearls. Such a shame. But all we really need is a strand of your hair, and we could have a million of you if we wanted. There will always be something missing, though. Your essence is what makes you. Plasma and amniotic fluid are two vital ingredients for life, but a soul can never be replaced."

The creature's gaze went to plants growing under fluorescent lights.

"Such as red grapes or okra plants. Those are added to the formula. The sap of plants can keep the tiny embryo alive for months, Samantha. Now we will have your eggs that Banth took and inseminate them by the most perfect specimen. You are the most important ingredient and will become food for your offspring."

I could feel tears one by one glide down my cheeks. As the creature spoke, I was once again in my mother and father's house in Pittsburgh playing with Lonny Horton, the boy next door, in the tree house my father built.

* * *

I remembered secretly playing with my Barbies for hours in my tree house. Lonny would sneak up so the other kids wouldn't make fun of him. I would keep his secret if he played with me.

"Sammy, why can't I ever be Barbie?"

"Because you're Ken. He's the dad, and Barbie's the mom."

"But I don't wanna be the dad."

"Lonny, I'm the mom. Next time you can be the mom."

"When I grow up, I don't ever want to be a dad."
"Oh, I want to be a mommy. I want tons of babies."

I picked up baby Skipper and put it in Barbie's arms.

* * *

The memory faded as the creature's low, raspy voice got loud, bringing me back to the present. "The technology here is all extra-terrestrial. Special lighting and construction to keep it an exact sixty degrees. Anything too warm or too cool will compromise the formula."

"You can't do this!"

"Ah...but we have." Banth suddenly appeared.

"You can't do this!"

"I see you met Obyzoutht."

"Let me go!"

"I gave you the opportunity to stay, but you declined my offer."

"You will be caught. Raul Roman has betrayed you! He and Agent Harmon are here. They will kill you, and if they don't, Lucien will find you and kill you."

He chuckled. "I don't think so. They are working with me."

"They're lying!"

"It is too late, Samantha. Your time is over. And I will raise your children and use their geno...after this planet is ours. And every human being will be enslaved or extinguished."

"You're mad!"

"The Mind Sweepers will be here soon. Take comfort in your surroundings, my dear." Banth left.

"Now, now, I will be a good mother to your children." Obyzoutht was upon me, laying a hand on my shoulder.

"Don't touch me." I cringed.

She was gone, leaving a black feather at my feet.

Tears exploded. I fell to the cement ground on my knees. The vats vibrated with their colors. The human bodies were still. The lights dimmed. No way out of this nightmare. My grief transformed into rage. Strength began to boil in me and light radiated from the darkness.

The ceiling was different from the rest of Dulce.

There were no drop-down beams. Banth said the ceiling was made using a special construction. I remember what Obyzoutht said. "Special lighting and construction to keep it an exact sixty degrees. Anything too warm or too cool will compromise the formula." There was no copper!

I held my hand out in front of me to point to the glass door. My palms began to glow. It shattered. I pulled my hands from the shackles, melting the steel within my grasp. I rubbed my wrists and stood and walked over to a large piece of the glass. I picked it up and held it up to my eyes. The reflection in the glass showed my glowing eyes, which looked the same as Lucien's.

"That's it. I am out of here."

18 MIND SWEEPERS

"Are we going to sit here debating or are we going to do this?" Lucien said.

"Let's move, before I change my mind," Tarragon said.

Gloria and Older smiled.

The door flew open, and Tarragon led the way. Lucien followed. They trotted through the hollow grim hallways to the rebellion.

"I'll get word to the alliance and the Fosters!" Rek said.

"How?" Tarragon halted in his tracks.

"I'll go to the communications station and try to hack the military's computer and send a signal!" Noah whispered.

"We should go to Perdition Seven where the Mind Sweepers are! They're the only ones who will go against Banth and the military."

Older waited for Lucien to answer.

"It may be our only hope," Gloria said.

"Wait...I have to think."

They were quiet a moment while Tarragon pondered.

"You think it's the best option?" The question was to Lucien. He didn't respond.

"It's the best solution to get word to the alliance and to the rest of your family. Agreed," Gloria said.

"Agreed," said Tucker.

"Agreed," said Noah.

"Agreed, dear friend." Older smiled.

"I hope you're right," said Tarragon. They all looked at Lucien.

"Agreed!"

Noah and Older took off to the communications center with their flashguns drawn, following Rek. A siren blared, and the overhead lights flashed on and off.

"All available personnel report to Level One possible breach," the voice over the loudspeaker said.

"It has to be Sam. The rebellion hasn't even begun."

Gloria grimaced.

"Not good," Tarragon said, facing her.

"You think it's Sam," Lucien said.

"No way to be sure unless we head there," Gloria said.

"We have to get the Mind Sweepers on our side. We have to take our chances there first."

"We might have enough time to get to Sam!" Gloria reached for Tarragon's arm.

"We have to try and bargain with the Mind

Sweepers first!"

"And, where are they?" asked Lucien.

"The Hall of Souls," said Gloria.

"We were already there, and she wasn't," Tarragon said.

"She may be hidden away with the keeper," Gloria said.

"No human or hybrid has ever been there lived to tell about it."

"There's always a first."

"I don't like this."

"We may be too late!" Lucien bellowed, his voice echoing through the tunnel. "What are we waiting for? Let's do this."

They made their way to the Hall of Souls.

* * *

"You smell that? It's sulfur," said Gloria.

"The smell is the keepers," Tarragon replied. "Obyzoutht."

Once inside the Mind Sweepers' domain, Lucien's thoughts were of Samantha. He could feel her there.

Gloria tiptoed to the broken shackles lying on the cement ground and picked them up. "She was here."

"We must have just missed her," Tarragon said.

"Yes. I can sense her thoughts," Lucien said.

He took the shackles from Gloria and rubbed them between his fingers. "Something is wrong.

She...I can't tell. Her thoughts are jumbled. I have to find her."

"At least we know she made it out of here alive."

"What is this place?"

"In those glowing tubes are the souls of the bodies hanging."

"Who did this?"

"Your government and the residents of Dulce."

"A high price to pay for technology."

"I've been here before, but I've never seen this level," Tarragon said. "They only want you to see what's in their best interests."

"Banth had Sam here; he was going to do this to her." Lucien's fist grew into tight balls of light.

"But they didn't. She's alive, and her mind is still intact," Gloria said.

"She must have seen that coming," Tarragon said.

"How do you know for sure? She may be here." Lucien walked up to the row of bodies.

"There are too many to search." Gloria's words were slow and solemn.

Lucien felt his anger well into despair. "I failed her."

"The metal had melted, and the shackles were broken. She somehow got away, Lucien."

A shrieking siren sounded. They held their ears.

Standing above them with their huge serpentine bodies and their saliva dripping from their mouths were the Mind Sweepers.

"Shit!" Lucien said through gritted teeth.

Two hovered over Lucien, Gloria, and Tarragon.

Gloria spoke first. "We n-need your h-help."

They cocked their alien heads. "We see. What makes you think we will help you?"

The creature dripped saliva on Lucien's boot. He looked down, lifting it, and grimaced.

"The hybrids and the humans are uprising against Banth," Tarragon said without fear.

"Why would we help you?"

Lucien stood in front of the alien.

"You have to help. You are alien and kept here to be Banth's slave and the military's. Is that what you want?"

"Not really," Banth said behind Lucien. Lucien turned.

"Seize them." Banth's guards grabbed Gloria. Tarragon used his flashgun on one of the Mind Sweepers.

"No, we need them," bellowed Lucien.

"Go!" Gloria wailed.

Tarragon raced out of the Mind Sweepers' quarry as fast as lightning. Lucien shot a beam of light from his palms, knocking Banth on the ground.

The Mind Sweepers lashed out at Lucien with a flashgun. He raised his brow and their weapons bended. Altering time, the walls began to twist and turn as he made his way through the greenish phosphorescent-glowing tunnels.

19 THE REBELLION

I stood over the empty incubator with tears streaming down my face. The other babies wailed at the sight of me. I looked around, wanting to save them from this place.

"People need to know what our government is doing here. Are any of them running the government even human?" I said out loud.

"My baby. I have to find you." Overwhelmed with the knowledge my baby was gone, I fought back more tears.

I exited the nursery, staring back one last time at the crying infants, and trudged through the large tunnels strung with lights. Drones began to awaken, and more sirens sounded.

I scurried to find Gloria and the rest of the Resistance. The closer I got to the upper levels, the louder the chaos. Shots began to fire. The rebellion was underway.

A dark haze of smoke enveloped the shafts. The air dusted with ash made me cough and catch my breath. I stopped to watch the cells on this level open and shut one by one. Making my way around a corner, I saw aliens and hybrids fleeing.

Sirens with red and blue lights blared through the corridor. I rushed, bumping into others running.

Foot soldiers whizzed by me, not taking notice of me. The crackling of steel rocked the walls. A large alien bolted into me, knocking me off my feet. I hurried to stand and gathered my wits hugging the wall. I stopped the first humanlike hybrid running near me.

"Can you tell me what cell Gloria's?"

"Banth's slave?"

"Yes!"

"Keep going. Hers is the last one near the elevator!" I began to run, making my way through panicking hybrids and human prisoners.

Gloria's cell was lit up. The sliding metal door opening and closing. I sneaked by before it shut.

"Gloria!" I slid to my knees. She was chained to the foot of her cot.

"Samantha! You're alive!"

"How long have you been like this?"

"Not long. We tried to find you."

"What's happening?"

"The military locked all the doors to the cells. But something must have knocked the power out."

My hands began to tremble, and strength rose within me like a bullet from a gun. Beams of light rose from my palms.

"The copper! How is that possible?"

"I don't know. But let's not stay here trying to figure it out." I broke the chains with my hands.

"How...did you...do this?"

"Long story. The copper shield must be compromised."

Gloria rubbed her wrists and stood. "Your Lucien is here. He's helping us."

"Banth was telling the truth."

"He got away with Tarragon! They found out that Noah and Rek and Older were helping me, but something tells me they succeeded. We tried to get the Mind Sweepers to help!"

"Some bitch named Obyzoutht has my baby!"

"The baby Banth needed a bone marrow transplant is yours?"

"Yes, mine and Lucien's. And there are more. I know it's complicated. Believe me, I have a hard time believing it myself." The lights were blinking on and off, and the door pounded open and close.

"We have to get out of here!"

"The firefight! Rek must have escaped with Tarragon."

"Let's go," I said.

I pulled on Gloria's arm.

When the door opened partway, we slid through.

Drones flew by. We ducked in between humans and hybrids.

The military were too busy to care. They were

running to the rebellion. The elevators doors were opening and closing just like the cell doors.

"How will we get to the upper levels?"

"The tunnels have an escape exit... a staircase if that happens," she said in a rushed breath of air.

"You serious? We have to climb through the tunnels!"

"Yes, but if the power's off, so is the air! We must hurry, Samantha. Just leave me here... I will never make...I'm too old. You go. While you have a chance." Gloria let go of my hand and coughed. I searched to my right and then to my left. Hybrids and humans tore through the tunnels, some knocking over the others, stomping over them. I watched in disbelief while Gloria caught her breath.

Smoke began to fill the tunnel, making it total chaos.

We ran as fast as our feet would allow. Then Gloria stopped, short of breath.

I waited for a second and pulled her along. She stopped again, taking in a deep breath. "Save yourself."

"No! I am not leaving you. We can make it. Take your top off."

She seemed confused. "Why?"

"Just do it!"

I helped her lift her top over her head.

"Cover your nose and mouth. Like this."

I wrapped her shirt around my nose and mouth.

"We can do this." I handed her back her shirt. She nodded and did what I told her to do.

We came to a rocky dead end. "This is it," Gloria said. "Push the rock. There's a lever. Do you see it?"

I knelt and felt the rough rock surface. "Found it." I hit the lever, and the rocky boulder moved back just enough for us to fit through.

We trudged up the narrow, dark, cobweb-infested stairwell. The smoke began to dissipate. Gloria stopped. I turned around, waiting.

"Fire must be out," she said.

"We have to be almost there. Move quickly."

"I don't know." She swallowed hard.

"I've never been here before."

I concentrated more on using my eyes as a flashlight.

Gloria stopped putting her top back on. Sweat poured from her face. I watched her as the lights flickered on and off.

"The lights," Gloria said.

"Thank God. Not sure how much longer I could keep that up." I was glad to see them. Using my eyes as a flashlight drained me.

"I still can't figure out how I can use my powers with the copper."

"Tarragon and the others must have found a way to breach the armor."

I took a breath. I felt my lungs expand with a weary and yawn, trying to lift my legs to move ahead.

Gloria hunched over.

"We can't stop," I said. "The air's stale."

She met my gaze.

"No, not the ventilation? This can't be happening."

"When the elevators shut down, so did the filters."

"What does that mean?"

"Exactly what you think it means."

"No air."

"We'll suffocate."

I scanned the stairwell's tunnel. No light shone through. Not even a hazy crack. Gloria started again and stopped.

"Just go without me."

"No. We can do this together."

"You are young and strong. You can get to the top before the air runs out."

I took her arm. "Gloria, you have to try."

She braced herself on my shoulder.

I took a breath. We took a few more steps, and she collapsed.

"Gloria, come on, we made it this far. Don't give up on me."

The air was thick and hot. I didn't hear the fans anymore, but the gunfire remained. I fell on my knees. Gloria hunched over on the carved-out step above me. She was breathing hard.

"You have to calm down. Breathing like that is

only going to make you weaker."

"Fans have shut down."

"I know. It's hot. Gloria, is there a backup generator?"

"Only on the main level. We're not going to make it, Samantha. We tried."

"No! I will not accept death in this godforsaken tunnel. Do you hear me! I will not die here."

A loud, explosive howl echoed through the shaft.

"What was that?"

"Is that what I think it is?"

A dog's barking echoed again, this time louder.

"Ruby! Oh my God, it's Ruby!"

The barking continued.

"Ruby girl, come!"

The barking got closer and closer. In a rush of air, Ruby toppled on me, licking me. "Gloria, it's Ruby. She's come to help!"

Gloria didn't move.

Ruby stood quietly, cocking her head.

"Ruby, get help!"

Ruby barked.

"Gloria, hold on, hold on!"

"Go find help!"

Ruby barked and licked her and turned and ran down the stairwell.

"Hurry, Ruby!"

20 TEN MINUTES

Pop, pop, pop. Shots were fired one after another. "How do you know who's on your side?" Lucien bellowed among the sirens and gunshots.

"It's like this: The Ultras, Maji, Alternative 3, and Orienis are alien," Tarragon said.

"The Watchers are the winged aliens, but they are fighting against us with Banth!" Rek bellowed over the siren and gunfire, running toward them.

Lucien held back a smirk while he loaded his gun. "They all look the same to me."

"We only have a few flashguns, so the human weapons will have to do. We were able to destroy the copper barrier controls."

Noah came running from a tunnel. Older was behind him, limping.

"Roman and someone named Harmon are loading their arms in the nursery!" Noah said.

"Harmon's here?"

"Do you know of him?'

"He's an Illuminati!"

"Whatever that is. He's with Roman," Noah said.

"Looks like embryos and laptops in there."

"The crowd's out of hand on the lower levels. And there's a fire!" Older said.

"I broke into the main station. The power has shut off." Rek shot a round of shots.

"Samantha is still there!"

"Foster, the fire is everywhere by now!" Rek said.

Tarragon shot his weapon, hitting two of Banth's soldiers.

"Gloria would try to get to a higher level."

"How do I get to Level One!" Lucien yelled.

"If Gloria knew the power was cut off, she would take the stairwell tunnel!" Older yelled.

"No one could survive in there with no air," Rek shouted over the gunshots.

"Not sure she if she realized the ventilation was compromised. She's a smart human, but she's old."

"Noah, you think you can take me to the stairwell?" Lucien asked.

"I think I can."

"You okay here?" Lucien shouted over the echoing gunfire and sirens to Tarragon.

"Go!"

"Make sure Gloria is with her. Promise me you will look for her if she's not with Samantha," Older said.

"I will."

Lucien and Noah scrimmaged through bloody aliens and human body parts scattered among the tunnels and ground. They maneuvered their weapons while running.

A huge scaffold went tumbling in front of Lucien. He jumped and rolled until he came to a tall Reptilian blocking his way.

"Well, Noah?" Lucien said, trying to get past the Reptilian. "Is he with the rebellion or not?"

Noah shrugged. "Your guess is as good as mine."

"You're kidding me!"

The alien did not move. He glared at Lucien with crimson-red eyes and a turned-up nose. Lucien decided to call his bluff.

"Seriously... I am on your side," Lucien yelled. The alien stopped and did a thumbs-up and ran.

They passed an open room with red beams of light, which caught Lucien's eyes.

"The alien artifacts laboratory. Banth's hobby!" Noah said. He gestured for Lucien to follow. "This way. Banth put in a secret door; it's faster than going through the main tunnel!" He surveyed the area. "I'm not sure this is the right place."

Lucien strode to a giant computer screen, showing a map of the whole complex. He picked up one of the artifacts.

"Come on; it's here."

"Wait, this resembles some type of key, maybe to an exit. If that's the case, we could use it. Look at this, do you know what it is?"

Noah walked over to see what Lucien was

looking at. He took the tiny device in his hand.

"Never seen it before."

"Okay, let's go, then."

"This way."

Lucien put it in his pocket.

They went through Banth's secret door to another level. Down two flights of stairs and out into the central hub.

They fled by cells with their doors banging open. Humans ran bleeding and screaming. A woman stopped and took Lucien's hand.

"Help us!"

"I can't... Noah, can you get her to the exit?"

More humans and small children appeared from cells, their hair shaggy and their faces smudged with dirt and ash.

"I have no alien powers like you." Sirens blared.

"I have to get to Sam!"

"Please help us!" the woman said in tears.

Lucien stood there a moment. He didn't have to think twice about it. He knew what he had to do. But the gnawing in the pit of his stomach saying "no" burned like a knife. He didn't want to help them. He wanted to save Sam and nothing more.

"Noah, which way to the stairwell?"

"Remember the room you were in when we found you?" Lucien nodded.

"Go there and find cell B. Once you are there, go to the Exit sign in red marked with an upside-down triangle with a black line through the center, then turn to your left. The stairwell is there under the overhead camera."

"Good—now find Sam!"

"Me?" He looked dumbfounded.

"Yes, you!"

"But..." Noah nodded and took off. Lucien looked at the woman and child.

"I'm all you got." He gave the woman a forced smile. "Okay?" The woman smiled and wiped her tears.

There are so many, he thought. Behind them, a thick cloud of smoke began to billow.

BANG.

He ducked, shielding the woman and child. The ceiling was beginning to come down.

All at once, his eyes glowed a florescent green, lighting up the underground compound. "Is everyone all right?"

They all nodded.

"All of you take each other's hand like this!" He took the young woman's hand. "Make a human chain!"

A voice from the rear said, "I'm a hybrid!"

"Okay, that's okay, just make a chain using your hands." He lifted his hands high, locked with the woman's hand. "Don't look back!"

They nodded and did what Lucien said, holding on to his every word. "Follow me and whatever you do, don't let go."

Lucien followed the exit signs to the upper level where the fighting was. The smoke and ash and crumbling pieces of the compound were overbearing his senses. The aliens were now fighting with the Resistance. This is where Banth and the government do their bidding, he thought. Small fires had broken out inside what had once had been offices and communications center. Tarragon, Rek, Older, came into view fighting through to an opening in the mountainside. Lucien watched Tarragon throw homemade bottle bombs one after another in the direction of Banth's Ultra 7 elite soldiers.

"Fire is one thing the Ultra Seven fear!" Rek yelled over the noise.

Lucien could feel the adrenaline rise within him as he made his way holding hands with the woman and the chain of others.

Tarragon did a double take. "Foster, what the hell are you doing?"

"Getting these humans to safety!"

Tarragon grimaced, ducking bullets.

"Can you get them out?" Lucien yelled.

"As soon as it's daybreak! The smoke is too heavy." The women and children hurried to Tarragon.

"Take it from here!"

"Where's Noah?"

"Trying to get to the stairwell to find Gloria and

Samantha in case I don't make it there!"

"There isn't going to be a stairwell, Foster. The Mind Sweepers set explosives!"

"How long do we have?"

Older shook his head. "Knowing the Sweepers, not long. I'm guessing fifteen minutes."

"That doesn't give us long. I'll have to alter time," Lucien shouted.

"The copper's out, so do it!"

"I know! How did you think I got this far?"

"I'm guessing you had no problem."

"I'll get these humans out to safety," Older said.

"No! I'll do it. Damn, you are too old! I'll lead you. Take the last human's hand." Lucien's eyes glowed, lighting up the tunnel.

"Foster, you have ten minutes." Tarragon threw a flashgun at Lucien. He caught it. "Not that you'll need it."

"Listen up, this is going to feel weird. Just hold each other's hand tight and don't let go. Older, that goes for you too, old man!"

"I'll old man you!" he said with a chuckle.

Lucien nodded and altered time. The walls moved in a spiral formation, leaning in and out. The fire was throughout the compound. The ceiling's steel beams and concrete fell around him as he raced with the human chain to the outside through the tunnels to the outside to Level One. Lucien got them as far as he could.

"Don't stop until you see daylight!"

"Go find your Samantha," Older said.

Lucien nodded and raced towards where Noah had told him the stairwell was.

Lucien came upon the red upside-down triangle. He turned to the left, and there were the camera and the entrance to the stairwell. Noah was standing there not moving.

"This is it. You're own your own. Not going anywhere with that creature staring me down!" Noah shrieked.

Ruby, full grown, was barking at the entrance to the stairwell, with her red eyes lighting up the rocky interior. Lucien stopped and focused. "Is that a dog?"

"What's a dog?"

"Yep. That's a dog. I have it from here! You don't have much time before this place goes up!"

Noah nodded and took off running.

Lucien and Ruby locked eyes.

"What you trying to tell me pup?"

"Help Human!"

"Sam!"

"Yes! Quick, no oxygen!"

Lucien ran to her. "Hey, girl, you know where Sam is, don't you?" Ruby barked.

Lucien followed her up the stairwell.

21 WAKE UP!

"Gloria, wake up," I said, taking shallow breaths. "Wake up."

"I'm not sleeping. I'm dying."

"No, you aren't. We...have...to...stay awake."

"Too tired."

A smoky haze enveloped me. More sirens sounded. I watched Gloria. She didn't move.

"More smoke..."

"I hope they...are...winning."

"Gloria, I am sorry. I wanted you to be free. At least for a little while."

"It's okay..."

"No, it's not."

"My life above wasn't a picnic."

"Anything is better than this." I tried moving. No strength. So sleepy. "We have to stay awake."

"There's no oxygen."

"Do you think they are searching for us?"

"Not while the...rebellion...is going on."

"Don't talk anymore. We have to conserve our oxygen."

"It's too late."

"You're right we are going to die here, aren't we, Gloria?"

She didn't answer.

All I could think of was what if my father never knew I loved him? He would always think I was either burned alive at Oakwood Estates or I just left. I would never see him again. Or the baby boy I would never hold again. And my Lucien.

I tried to move the dust on the step with my mind. Nothing. I tried to make my eyes light up the stairwell. Nothing.

I tried again. Nothing. No air. No air. I was dying.

The stairwell shook with a loud howl. "Ruby!"

I felt wet kisses on my cheek.

"Sam!"

I heard my name.

"Samantha!"

Ruby's bark.

Ruby.

"Sammy!"

Who was calling my name? Was I dead?

"Samantha, Samantha, baby, wake up. It's me, Lucien." He was patting my cheeks. More wet kisses. I opened my eyes. Ruby was licking my face. "Samantha, wake up. I turned on the generator. You should start to feel better, baby."

Ruby sat down next to Lucien.

"Ruby girl, you found Lucien. I never thought I would hear your voice again."

Ruby barked.

"Gloria. Is she all right?"

I felt Lucien's presence leave me.

"She's fine but weak."

"Where does this stairwell lead, Gloria?"

She didn't reply for a moment. "The top. The helicopter pad."

"Rest a moment."

A breeze wafted through my hair. "The fans are working," I said.

"Noah must have gotten to them."

"Gloria, you hear that?"

"Lucien, I can move things with my mind just like you." I smiled.

Lucien moved the hair from my eyes. "You can?"

He cradled me in his lap while the oxygen-filled my lungs. "I have so much to tell you."

"I thought I'd never see you again."

"I have to tell you—"

"We have to move. There are explosives about to go off at any moment." He lifted me and then lifted Gloria's arm over his shoulder. "Ladies, I know you are weak, but we have to move and quick. And that includes you, Ruby." She barked.

The stairwell began to shift into a spiraling wind tunnel that took us.

I knew what was happening. Time-shifted and slowed so we could make it to the top. Just when our feet touched the surface and daylight shone on our eyes, blinding me, an explosion rocked the mountainside. The structure trembled.

Gloria stumbled, taking me with her on the final step leading to the ground above us. Lucien caught me before I fell.

"We made it," I said to Gloria, embracing her. "You're free! I never thought I would ever love the smell of the New Mexico desert before in my life." I shielded my eyes from the bright sunlight. Being underground so long, it took me a while to get used to it. Gloria covered her eyes, not opening them. She began to cry.

"The sun...the sun," she said, holding on to me for dear life.

The mountaintop was covered in smoke and human and alien hybrids. A helicopter flew overhead, blowing dust and our hair wildly. The chaotic scene unraveled before me. From the central hub, the president and his entourage ran to board a plane. Banth watched us. Evil poured from his pores.

"Stop them, I said!"

Ruby's ears went into alert mode. She pounced on the president's leg and didn't let go. His leg went in all directions. "Get this mutt off me," he bellowed.

"He's behind it all. All of it. He's one of them!" I

yelled.

The president met my gaze.

Then a woman ran from the rocky exit of Dulce. She sprinted near the small plane, holding a baby.

"O'Neil! She has my baby!" I broke free from Lucien.

"*Baby?*" Lucien said, looking in the baby's direction.

"Our baby." The wind from the helicopter blew my hair in front of my eyes, making it impossible to see his expression.

I pulled my hair off my face, trying to see his reaction. He and I stared at each other as if time stopped.

He finally spoke. "I don't understand."

"That's what I wanted to tell you!"

O'Neil stopped in her tracks. Rek lunged for her. She turned the other way and started to run to the helicopter.

"Give me back my baby, bitch!"

Ruby let go of the president's leg, growled, and went after O'Neil.

Gloria ran en route to her and struggled with O'Neil, took the baby, and ran.

Pop, pop, pop. More shots. Gloria stopped. Her attention gave way to me. I hurried and took the baby from her before she fell to the ground. Lucien stopped her and laid her down.

"She's hit in the shoulder! he yelled.

"My son. You're safe." She looked at Banth, O'Neil, and the president. Lucien gazed into her gray-blue eyes.

"Your son," he said.

"Yes..."

I kept my distance, watching the two. I held my tears back. "You're my mother?" Lucien said with shock in his tone.

"I don't understand."

Another helicopter landed, blowing debris.

She lifted her head and turned to Banth and the president and spoke. "What you did was wrong," she shouted over the sound of the chopper's blades. "What you all did was wrong. It has to end here and now."

"You're right, it has to stop." It was Jordan Taylor. With him was Nathan Moore coming from the helicopter.

The fire was taking over Dulce. Tarragon, Noah, and Older came running through the mountainside's exit.

"You're a stupid human! The babies in the nursery are yours as well!" O'Neil said, speaking to me.

"You're lying!" I said.

"What babies?" Lucien turned to me.

"They can't be!" I yelled.

"There are more!" O'Neil said.

"The Mind Sweeper set a bomb! We have to

leave now!" Older yelled.

"We can't save them!" Tarragon said.

"We have to!" My eyes met Lucien's.

"This is way too much." He raked his hand through his hair, surveying the mess in front of him. Women and children cried. Smoke surrounded us all. More aircraft were landing.

"When we were in the Aurora's Curtain...They took my eggs!"

"I thought that was a hallucination. It was real?"

"They're going to destroy Earth and repopulate with my DNA."

"A virus is already killing off the humans," Older said.

"Lucien, we can't let them die!" I implored.

"How much time do we have?"

"Not long. Hurry, this way!" Rek said.

Lucien followed.

"How many?"

"Maybe ten!" I said.

Nathan Moore grabbed O'Neil and held a gun to her head. "How many?"

She glared at Lucien with her olive eyes. Nathan pulled her ponytail, making her neck snap back.

"A dozen maybe!"

He let her go. Jordan took the gun.

"Let's go! Come on!" Noah said. "We haven't much time!" Nathan followed the others.

"Carry as many as you can hold," Lucien said.

Ruby barked.

Tarragon, Noah, Nathan, and Rek raced to the opening in the mountainside.

Older sat down next to Gloria, cradling her in his arms. I settled near them.

Lucien ran to my side. "If for any reason, we don't make it—"

"No, stop. You will. You have to make it."

Lucien kissed me. He gazed at the baby a moment and turned and followed the others. I watched him, and the others run, moving to the mountain.

The women, men, and children abductees scattered and moved fast in the direction of the pathway to the desert.

The Mind Sweepers were the last to emerge from the tunnel. Their main objective was to take care of Banth. He was just about to board the plane when the Mind Sweepers started for him. O'Neil pushed the arm Jordan had with the gun. It fired, hitting one of the Mind Sweepers. She ran toward him, pushing Banth in the plane just in time before the other Mind Sweepers got him. The plane took off down the pad.

"Come back!" yelled the president, searching the sky. More choppers and Jeeps filled with Division Six landed.

Landson Shaw from Greenbrier came rushing from a chopper. "You're safe, thank God!" he said.

"Landson..."

"This is what they wanted!"

He gazed at the baby.

"They intended much more," I said.

"Where's Lucien, and Moore?"

"Inside. There are more babies."

"You're kidding me!"

"I wish I was."

More choppers flew overhead.

"The vice president!" I watched the Secret Service take the president away. I held my tiny baby tight.

"They better hurry," Older said.

Gloria began to cough, then nothing.

"Gloria, Gloria," Older yelled. He laid her flat. "I think it's her heart."

"What?" I said and handed Older the baby. I slid to my knees. "Gloria, can you hear me?" She didn't respond. I checked her pulse.

"Her heart stopped."

I tilted her head back. "She's not breathing."

Older backed up and gave me room. "I'm going to start compressions!" I laid my hands on her chest and started CPR. "One, two, three, four," I counted to thirty and breathed twice. Older, Jordan, and Landson Shaw watched. I started to get light headed when Landson Shaw eased me out of the way and started doing compressions. Gloria moaned.

"Oh, thank God!"

Jordan took her pulse. "Nice and steady."

He checked the gunshot. "She needs a hospital."

Tarragon was the first to arrive at the opening in the mountain. He had two infants. Noah ran with two in his arms along with Rek, who had a cart carrying four infants. Moore had his arms full of two.

Lastly, Lucien carried two.

Jordan handed the gun over to a Division Six agent and walked briskly with his cane, headed for Lucien. He took one of the babies.

"The mountainside is going to go up any second," Tarragon said.

Lucien gave me the baby he was holding.

"Go to her," I said. "We had to do CPR on her. She may crash again."

Lucien ran over to Gloria. He took Gloria and cradled her in his lap. "Give them a moment," I said to Older.

I watched Lucien cradle Gloria. The first and last time he would probably share with the mother who would never know her son. I felt a tear well. I hurriedly wiped it away. I gazed down at the baby in my arms, grateful they were safe.

"Sam, Lucien, this mountainside is going up and fast," Nathan Moore yelled.

"Leave me, Lucien," I heard Gloria say.

"No...I can't."

"This is right. This is the only home I've known. The only home in so many years. As horrible as it was. This is all I've known. I want to die here."

Lucien laid her down. Older came up behind them giving him the baby.

"I'll stay with my old gal." He sat down on the ground and laid Gloria's head in his lap.

"We can take you both to the ranch. Jordan, tell them," Lucien pleaded.

"No! Go with Samantha and my grandchildren." Lucien grimaced as Ruby barked.

"Go," Gloria said.

Lucien took one last look at Gloria.

"This is so wrong on all levels," I said.

"We have to hurry..." Nathan said.

A huge army helicopter landed.

"They will take you to Greenbrier—it's a safe place," Nathan said to Tarragon, Tucker, Noah, and the others. "There are others like you there."

Three more helicopters landed.

"We'll take the hybrids to Greenbrier," Landson Shaw said.

"What about the virus?" I asked.

"The CDC is working with our top infectious disease experts. Until it's contained, we will quarantine."

I took the baby from Lucien.

Before we boarded the helicopter, I held my baby tight with Ruby at my feet and watched Division Six agents carry the babies onto the chopper, boarding first. My gaze shifted to Older and Gloria. I wiped a stray tear from my face. Jordan gestured for us to board next. We climbed aboard just in time. Flames shot out in all directions from the entrance to the underground compound. I turned my face, not wanting to see Older and Gloria.

Dust and smoke flew into the horizon. The sky was painted with dark gray clouds. Lucien stared out the chopper window.

I wish I had the gift of telepathy so I could know how Lucien was really handling all of this. Gloria and Older began to turn into fuzziness among the fog and smoke as the plane flew away, and so did the image of Dulce. The memory faded as we departed, flying off to the sky.

22 FEVER

"Oh my God, they are precious," Eden said, cradling one of the babies in her arms. Ruby barked at Eden. Her hair flared out on her back.

"Be nice, Ruby," I said, petting down her hair.

"Dog, be quiet."

Eden gave me a wicked smile.

"Ruby's her name."

Her eyes glowed red.

"She's a hybrid. One of Dulce's better experiments."

"Lovely! Just keep her away from me."

"Eden, you don't like dogs?" Of course, she doesn't.

Foster Ranch looked more like a nursery than housing for highly intelligent ETs.

"Eden rushed out to Walmart and got pop-up cribs, diapers, onesies, bottles, formula, binkies, and stuffed animals. What do you think of that?" Michael said.

"That was very kind of you."

"Well, someone had to do it."

"And you loved it," Michael said.

Eden didn't say anything. I think she liked being a bitch more.

"Do you think you bought enough baby stuff?" I said, picking up an unboxed activity gym.

"Jordan called and said there were babies and to get supplies. So, I got supplies."

"Yes, you did."

Michael held one of the babies, Gabe another, and Jordan rocked one. Nathan had two. Daniel was giving one a bottle while the others slept. Lucien wheeled the others in a wagon into the infirmary.

I took in a breath, feeling overwhelmed. The quiet hum of Foster Ranch made me miss the young, naive girl who stepped out the secret elevator wide-eyed. I could almost hear Cassiel's voice mocking me.

"You still are."

There he was, the smart-alecky Cassiel. A huge smile brimmed his handsome face. "Just as long as you come when you're invited."

Eden cocked her head at me.

I didn't respond. This was going to be my little secret for now. I laid this baby down and glanced at the little boy in my arms.

"He looks like Mom," Finn said over my shoulder.

"Too young to tell."

"He does!" Finn said.

"Too young to tell what?" Eden said, seeming confused. Jordan smiled like he knew my secret.

Lucien came up from behind and wrapped his arms around me.

"I wish Gloria would have come with us. We could have saved her." Lucien struggled to get the words out.

"She seemed to be strong-willed," Jordan said.

"This doesn't make sense. She was human," I said.

"Some things are better left unknown, don't you agree?" Jordan said.

"We're part human?" Lucien said. He looked at his brothers.

Michael, Gabe, and Daniel all grimaced.

"There are a lot of unanswered questions, I know. Just be patient. Let's not rush to judgment until the Division, and I delve deeper into it," Jordan said.

Michael gave him half a nod.

"Unless they used her womb as an incubator," Lucien said.

"We can do a DNA test. I am sure we can find a hair or remains," Nathan said.

"No...we should just live our lives as we have been doing," Michael said.

"What difference does it make?" Daniel walked over to one of the cribs and laid down the sleeping infant.

"How are we going to take care of twelve infants?"

Eden glared at her uncle. "We aren't."

Lucien took his baby in his arms. "Sam, they are your eggs. But who knows who the father is? Can you live with the thought of Banth being the father?"

"I never thought of that." I gazed at the babies in front of me.

Lucien wrapped his hand around mine. "We know for sure this one is yours and mine, but the others?"

"Won't a DNA test prove you are the mother?" Michael said.

"It may, but how on Earth would you be able to care for hybrids?"

"There is no way of telling what they are capable of until they are grown. You saw what Dusty could do."

I remembered Dusty. The sneakers he caught on fire and Oakridge. And Cassiel's boot outside the corral. The thought of Gabe wearing that fire-resistant suit when he taught Dusty how to control his gift of pyrokinesis.

"Uncle, when did you learn what we could do?"

"Your abilities were subtle until you were into puberty."

"We can have Landson Shaw take them to Greenbrier," Nathan said.

"Isn't there any other option?" I asked.

"We'll discuss this later. You need to rest now, especially my grandchildren." Jordan smiled and left us.

"I guess he's referring to us."

Lucien's siblings smiled and followed Jordan.

"Jordan, hold up, I want a word with you," Nathan said.

"Follow me into my office."

We stayed a moment with the babies.

"I think we should take Nathan's advice and call Landson Shaw."

"I know...They're right. It's just so hard to let them go. It's the most practical thing to do. How could we care for them the way they need to be cared for? Go ahead make the arrangement to take the babies to Greenbrier," I said with a heavy sigh.

"Tomorrow."

* * *

I became attached to the baby I rescued in the nursey at Dulce. I laid him on Lucien's bed. His little arms and legs sprang out while I rushed to change his diaper. Before I knew it, he was peeing all over Lucien.

Lucien lifted his shirt over his head and stripped down to his boxers. "Give me the little sprout."

Lucien began to undress the baby. "What are you doing?"

He picked up the infant, went into the bathroom, and opened the shower door.

"You're going to scare him!"

"Nah. He's tough like his mom." He gently rinsed the baby off. I handed him a washcloth and soap.

I watched Lucien clean his baby. Before I knew it, I was in the shower with him. He bent down and kissed me. The warm water washed my fears, doubt, and anxiety away. The two most beautiful creatures I had ever seen were staring back at me. Lucien stepped out and handed me the baby and draped a towel around us. He took the baby while I put on a robe and took a white linen towel and wrapped the baby in it.

I gazed at the bundle in my arms, taking in his sweet scent.

We walked over to the bed. Lucien took the baby from me. He handed me a diaper, and I put it on the best I could.

"Not bad for the first time."

"Thank Eden for rushing out before we got back," I said.

Lucien struggled with a sleeper.

"How the heck does his little arms fit in this contraption without breaking them?"

"Carefully!"

I wrapped a blanket tightly around the baby and laid him on his back in a pop-up crib.

"There, all cozy," Lucien said.

"We will have to get him a proper crib."

"This is fine for now."

Lucien took my hand, and we lay on the bed next to the crib, gently so as not to disturb the baby. "Banth had him the whole time. Did you know that?"

"You remember?"

"They took my memory, but Banth gave it back to me."

"You remember everything?"

"Everything."

His lips met mine.

"I've longed for those days on the ship," Lucien said.

"Banth didn't call it that. He called it the Black Knight."

"He called it that. He told me something crazy about the Black Knight."

"Why didn't you tell me when you first came back, or on the highway?"

"That's what I tried to tell before you got shot in West Virginia. I was stuck in a maze in the Aurora's Curtain."

"You weren't stuck. Dr. O'Neil purposely put you there. To by time. We were happy. It was a whole different world in whatever it was."

"Had I known what Banth was up to..." Lucien whispered.

"They created what we wanted to see. Was any of it real?"

"It was a virtual reality, a matrix."

"Like the place in Dulce. Banth created to try and trick me into staying there with him."

"He tried to trick you with his illusions."

"He tried. But it was so real, just like when were taken up by the light. It was a community with people, cities, and oceans."

"It wasn't real."

"It couldn't have been all fake. It all happened. Banth let me remember."

"It was an optical illusion, Sam."

"I remember making our son. How do you explain that?"

"That...may be true."

"Maybe? Lucien, I remember. Why do you doubt it?"

"Because Banth would do anything to deceive us."

A second of silence passed.

"It seemed like we were there for years."

"Only a few human days, if that." There was a scratch at the door. Lucien got up and answered the door. "Ruby!"

She settled on the ground next to the crib.

"What was she like?" Lucien asked. His eyes glazed over.

"Gloria?"

He nodded.

"She was brave. Taken so young. She lived there

all those years underground. Exposed to all Banth's horrors."

"I would have liked to have known her."

I wanted to ask him so many things, like what happened after the firefight in West Virginia, but I had to let him mourn the mother he would never know.

Lucien peered over at the baby "We have to name him."

I thought a moment. "Ory?"

Ruby barked.

My son smiled like he could read my mind.

"It's perfect. What do you think?"

"Ory?"

"Gloria means glory. Ory sounds like Glory."

Lucien looked at me a moment. "Ory?" He studied my expression and raised an eyebrow. He took the baby's finger, and the baby grasped his finger.

"What do you think? You like Ory?"

"He loves it!"

My thoughts drifted to my father. "How am I going to explain this to my dad?" It was obvious by Lucien's expression he was worried as well.

"We will have Jordan invite him to the ranch. Explain to him what has happened. Nathan Moore can be here."

"It will have to work. How long have I been gone?"

"It may have seemed like forever, but it wasn't."

"Thank God."

Lucien cringed like he was in pain. "You okay?"

"Yeah, just felt strange a moment."

I took his hand and squeezed it. "They took my bone marrow."

"Yes, that's what Gloria said."

"Has Jordan examined him?"

"He will. After he rests."

We both gazed at our baby sleeping baby.

"If we give Landson the other babies, will he be able to tell who their biological father is?"

"Sam, they are a mixture of who knows what."

"But—"

"No...we can't. Landson will make sure they survive."

Tears began to well in my eyes.

Lucien pulled me to him as close as he could.

"I couldn't stop thinking of you," I said.

"I love you, Sam. More than ever. I just wished things were different. I want you to experience what we shared when Ory was conceived."

"I want that too."

I longed for his touch more than ever. He lowered my chin and kissed me. Just as I remembered.

We kissed like we hadn't seen each other in years. His warm kiss, gentle but wanting. Like our lives depended on it. My fingers gripped his hair, pulling him closer. My heart pounded wildly in my chest, and every vein expanded. I had never wanted anyone like this before. He pushed me backward on the bed. His body on top of mine felt mystical. I felt him for the first time—all of him—pressed against me. I inhaled his scent I remembered, the smell of the fire gone. The most delicious aroma of vanilla and cinnamon I could ever imagine. I wanted to breathe in all of him. His lips tasted of honey. His face had the slightest bit of stubble, and it scratched my skin, but I didn't care. I didn't care at all except for him. He felt wonderful. His hands explored everywhere, and it didn't matter that his mouth had already pressed against mine. I wanted him closer, closer, closer. He was and always would be my everything.

I suddenly understood why people said lovemaking was like becoming one because every inch of my body dissolved into his. We stayed there intertwined until the baby cried.

"Can you believe that sound is our baby crying?"

"No." Lucien smiled and lifted himself off me. He pulled his jeans up and went over to the baby.

I lifted myself up and scrambled for my panties and stood.

Lucien picked up Ory. He wailed as Lucien tried to comfort him. "He's burning up!"

"What!" I rushed to him and touched Ory's forehead. "He's sick. What did Banth do to him?" I cried.

Lucien placed his hands on the baby. A spectrum of light radiated from his hands. I stood close to him.

"Nothing is happening. Why?"

"I don't know. Whatever is going on with him, it's not from this planet." Lucien rocked the baby back and forth as he paced.

"We have to take him to Jordan."

23 BANTH'S VIRUS

No sound could be heard from the lab except the rhythmic hum of the hydrogen water-purification filters. My heart fluttered while Jordan examined baby Ory. My head pounded. I had a hard time focusing while I looked on.

The fresh air was blowing, but I was sweating.

Eden brought Jordan a thermometer. He gently placed it in Ory's ear while he screamed. "Are any of the other babies exhibiting anything similar?"

"No, they are fine," replied Eden.

"What's wrong with him?" I asked.

Lucien wrapped his arm around me.

"Well, it's obvious he sick," Eden said brashly.

"You know what, Eden? I don't need your rude comments."

"Ladies, come on. Let's be civil," Michael said.

Finn appeared.

"Sammy...it's going to be okay." I could tell by Finn's worried exterior he was just as concerned as me. I never told anyone I could see dead people. I wasn't about to tell them now.

"Is it Banth's manufactured virus?" I asked.

"Can't know for sure."

The room began to spin. I hadn't felt this way since I drank too much of my dad's Jack Daniels, and this time, I wasn't drunk.

I staggered.

"Sam, you okay?" Lucien said.

"She's going down!" Michael sounded like his words were coming from a Coke bottle.

Before I knew it, I went crashing down on the cold tile floor. "Sam!" I heard Lucien echo through a tunnel.

"Her breathing is labored," Jordan said. I felt him take my wrist.

"Pulse is weak. Get her to the bed next to the baby!"

Lucien picked me up like I was a Raggedy Ann doll. My arms hung limply at my sides. He laid me down on a bed in the infirmary.

"What's wrong with me?" I said.

"Whatever Ory has, you have it too," Michael said, placing a cool rag on my forehead.

"Sam, I am going to test some of your blood to see what we are dealing with," Jordan said. He wrapped a band on my forearm, and the needle went in. But nothing was coming out. "She's dehydrated."

He took the band off my arm.

"Samantha, I am going to try your hand, okay? It's going to hurt." I nodded.

He pricked me again. This time, blood began to

flow.

"This may be nothing but exhaustion and dehydration."

"Or Dulce." Lucien grimaced.

"It could be any virus from the pit," Eden moaned. "And now we all have the possibility of contracting it, thanks."

"Should we quarantine?" Lucien asked.

"Everyone calm down!" Jordan said.

"If it's a virus, it's too late for that. But something tells me this is not airborne." Jordan listened to my heart.

"Get Nathan; we need to get hold of Landson. We have to get the other babies to safety."

"Just take care of Ory. I will fight this."

Daniel came running in; with him was Nathan Moore. "Sam, you sick?"

"It appears to be that way," Jordan said, taking the stethoscope earpiece out.

"We both are," I said, looking at Ory.

"Division Six terminated most of the aliens that were hostile. Maybe they emitted the virus when they were killed."

"They did?" Gabe said. "Was that wise?"

"We didn't have much of a choice."

"The explosion destroyed everything. If there was an antidote, it's gone."

"Is anything going to happen to the president?" Michael said.

Nathan Moore shook his head. "They can't prove anything."

"Bullshit!"

"What about the Hybrids, Tucker, Tarragon, and Noah?" I said.

"They were taken to Greenbrier until we can place them."

The baby screamed and screamed, then he quieted.

"Lucien, Nathan and I would like to speak to you privately," Jordan said.

I watched them intently. This was not good. What were they going to talk about?

"We are going right in the next room. Don't worry, Sam."

He left with a worried expression.

I tried moving the glass on the counter. Nothing. I tried pushing the chair with my mind. Nothing. My alien powers were gone.

I tried to get up. My head throbbed, but I tried.

"What are you doing?" Eden came rushing over.

"I want to see what they are talking about."

"No, you don't. You need to lie down." She settled near the baby.

I tried to focus despite the black spots blocking my vision. I waited while they had their meeting without me. Eden stayed by the baby's side. I thought back to Dulce. Who knows what they did to me there? It was filthy. The needle they used to remove my bone marrow might have been contaminated with something. But that would not explain why my baby was ill.

Jordan and the boys came back.

Their faces were long and their steps slow. The room suddenly became grim. "What is it..."

I lifted myself up, threw my legs over the bed, and stood.

"Until we know what we are dealing with, you have to lie down. Both your temperatures are sky-high, Sam," Jordan said.

"I'm okay, just a little woozy."

"No, you're not," Lucien said.

I started to collapse.

Lucien rushed to my side. "Sam!" He caught me.

My heart was beating wildly in my chest. Their faces gray.

Jordan took a blood pressure cuff and put in on my arm. I watched him pump the cuff up and listen to my pulse. "Fifty-six over forty-five."

"No wonder she's light-headed," Michael said.

"Sam, I am going to find out what is making you and the baby ill. It may take a little bit of time, but I am going to find out," Jordan said.

"Is it the virus Banth and his cronies concocted to knock off humanity?" Gabe said.

"No, they got that under control with a vaccine, but there are more coming," Jordan said.

"Jesus Christ," Nathan said.

I watched Lucien cringe again.

"Lucien's ill!"

"No, I am fine,"

Jordan took his wrist to feel his pulse.

"Lucien, what are you feeling?"

"Nothing, I'm just worried."

"This is something different," Nathan said.

"Then what is it?" I asked. Their expressions showed more than simple concern. They were worried.

"It may be your body's rejecting Lucien's blood," Michael said.

"Why now?" I said.

"Or you caught a virus from Dulce."

"That makes more sense since the baby has it."

"Any of the other babies experiencing anything?" Gabe touched Ory.

"They're fine," Eden said.

"We have no idea what they were cooking down there."

"Rest assured, we will find out what it is," Jordan said.

A moment passed, and he and the rest turned and walked from the infirmary.

"We're going to try and get some answers from the Division, get some shut-eye." Nathan said in a reassuring voice.

He headed for the elevator.

Lucien ambled over to shut the door and sat

down on the bed next to me. I felt my energy leave me and my eyes went heavy.

"What's happening to me?"

He took my hand in his. "It's going to be okay," he said, caressing my hand.

I couldn't keep my eyes open. I tried to focus and stay awake. I felt Lucien leave me and slowly walk over to the cradle and gaze at Ory. His visage began to get fuzzy as my eyes closed.

24 SAVING HER

"How will we tell her?" Lucien said, hunched over on the table in the dining hall.

"Why don't you wait until Nathan comes back?" Jordan Taylor squeezed his nephew's shoulder. Lucien wiped tears from his face and stood.

His fists turned into tight balls.

"I want to kill him with my bare hands. Rip him limb to limb!"

"I know you do."

"It was all for nothing. Everything. Saving her, recusing her. Cassiel was right all along. I should have let her die."

"No! You had to do it." Eden rushed in.

"It's what you wanted from the beginning."

"What you did, Lucien saved you!"

He grimaced and raised his hand, gesturing for her to leave.

"Saved me, saved me? What from—a life of loneliness? Never knowing what it's like to be human. To love just to lose it? You don't know what you're saying. You have no idea."

"But I do, Lucien."

Michael scowled at her. She lowered her head.

His brother Daniel came rushing in. He waved papers in his hand. "We have a connection with Moira."

Lucien began to laugh, not just a normal chuckle. He went to a full-fledged roar.

"Are you mad?" Gabe said.

"What's so hilarious, Brother?" Michael smiled showing cautious curiosity. Lucien took a few deep breaths and sat down to catch his breath.

"Moira?" he said calmly and thought back to what Banth said at Dulce. "It doesn't matter," Lucien said.

"What doesn't matter?" Michael said.

"Any of it."

"Yes, it does," Daniel added.

"Moira doesn't exist," Lucien said.

"Yes, it does. Where's this coming from?" Jordan said.

"The Black Knight."

Everyone eyeballed each other except for Lucien. He was still. Silence swept through the room like the power shut off.

"How do you know about the Black Knight?" Michael said.

"Banth."

"Rubbish," Jordan said.

Lucien knew Daniel always tried to keep the

peace between them whenever there was conflict.

"It the mother ship from Moira who took us through the light."

Daniel interrupted. "Lucien, help me with the satellite."

Eden put her hand on Lucien's shoulder. He didn't react.

He kept his attention on his uncle.

"You best go calibrate the satellite with Daniel," Jordan said.

"Brother, you need the fresh air. Help me."

Daniel gave Jordan a nod. "He'll be ok. I got this."

Lucien paused a moment, locking eyes with his uncle. He knew the Black Knight was real. What he didn't know was—what was Banth talking about and what did it have to do with him.

Lucien kicked up his feet and followed Daniel outside to the satellite. Both were quiet. Lucien climbed up the steps while Daniel hit the switch, raising the large flashlight to the sky and doing a 180-degree turn. Daniel was giving him instruction when a dark sedan pulled up fast, gravel skipping with it. The door opened.

"Here it is!" Nathan Moore bellowed.

Lucien jumped down from the ladder and rushed to Nathan's side. Daniel was right behind him.

"What did you find out?"

Eden followed and stood next to Lucien.

"Here it is." Moore handed Lucien a file.

Daniel intercepted it and opened it to read the first paragraph. And stopped. He stood there speechless.

Eden took the file from his hand and began to read.

"This isn't possible!"

"What you are talking about?" Lucien took the file. His hands began to tremble as he began to read. "It's an option. Otherwise..."

Nathan grimaced.

Lucien felt like he was kicked in the groin. Every ounce of air left his body.

Eden slowly took the file from her brother. "Why is this happening?"

"Because we don't belong here. We never did," Daniel replied.

Jordan stepped out the front door. "What's going on out here?"

The rest of the Foster Clan met Nathan Moore.

"It's a virus," Nathan Moore said.

"The one that's killing half the populations?" Michael said.

"No, they're spreading that through the chemtrails."

"Then what?" Eden asked.

"This one was manufactured in Dulce. Most likely from one of the species in captivity at Dulce."

"Make an antidote. Simple." Jordan's shaking leathery hand took the file from Eden.

"If it were that simple." Nathan rubbed his brow. "No one at Division has seen anything remotely like it before."

"Well then, now they have. Get the most brilliant scientist on it. Right away. Any amount of money, take it from my office vault and use it."

A late-afternoon haze enveloped the ranch. The air was warm, and a breeze wafted through the Fosters and Moore while they spoke.

Lucien's mind was a million miles away. He thought back to the ship and how happy he and Sam were waiting for the baby to be born. And now this. He saw their lips moving, but he was miles away. It was like he was watching a movie without the volume up.

"Jordan." Nathan shook his head. "There is no antidote on Earth. They have no idea what type of alien virus it is. What we do know is that both the baby and Sam have it. I know this is grim. But we must accept the reality of it.

"I know a well-recognized physician and biochemist in Europe." He turned to leave. "I'll get in touch with him. Hold tight until I return," Nathan said.

The surreal feeling left Lucien and reality once again hit.

"Hurry, Moore," Jordan yelled.

"Uncle, what don't you understand? They're dying. And there is no cure or any antidote!" Lucien let out an agonizing bellow.

"I'm dying?" Samantha said.

Everyone turned.

She was holding on to the front door frame. The pallor of her skin took his breath away. He watched her hands tremble.

"Sam…We will find a cure. I promise."

Michael hurried and took hold of her.

She turned to him and whispered, "Why is he lying?"

"We all deal with bad news a different way."

Lucien swallowed hard, taking her from Michael and wrapping her arm around his shoulder to help her back inside.

* * *

Jordan and Nathan were at the whiteboard doing equations while Eden and Gabe, alongside Michael, were busy face-timing a panel of scientists at the Division Six hideaway.

Minute by minute, Sam and the baby continued to get weaker. Lucien spent every second by her side watching her slip away. The baby snuggled next to Sam, who was trying to get him to take a bottle.

"He won't eat." Tears streamed down Samantha's cheek.

Ory's small lips sucked the nipple of the bottle, and then he turned his cheek.

"He's going to die, Lucien, isn't he?"

Lucien wiped Sam's tear. "No... Jordan is working with the Division; they'll think of something. You got to believe that, Sam. Don't give up."

Ruby stayed by Sam and the baby's side while others brainstormed and annotated.

"Here, take him," Samantha said, collapsing on the pillow while tears fell down her cheek.

Lucien grimaced, holding Ory close to his chest. He left her side and opened the door, turning back one last time before he slowly closed the door to let her sleep.

He stood watching her through the glass of the infirmary. Jordan saw his pain and stood next to him.

"I can't take this, Uncle."

"I know, son."

"Why is this happening?"

"If I had the answers to why horrible things happen, I'd be a wealthy man."

"You're already a wealthy man." Lucien raised his brow and gave him a smile.

He returned the smile.

"Well, I'd be wealthier."

"This is Banth's fault. Going underground to Dulce was too much for her human body."

"They'll be here soon to take the babies back to Greenbrier."

"So soon?" Lucien gazed at the baby sleeping in his arms.

Lucien opened the infirmary's door and went back inside Samantha's room and laid Ory in the crib.

He watched Samantha until he felt for sure she was asleep. He softly walked out of the infirmary, leaving her.

* * *

Dusk fell on Foster Ranch, leaving its somber blanket upon it. The humming of the water filters purred through the underground dwelling.

Daniel interrupted the calm before the storm. "They're here. Landson Shaw just pulled up behind the van," Daniel said, focusing on the security camera monitor. "Three women just got out. You ready to do this?" He gazed at Lucien.

"I'm not waking her."

"For the best."

Lucien, Michael, and Gabe took as many babies as they could carry to the van.

Eden handed one of the babies to one of the women. She wiped a tear. "They will need to eat in two hours. Make sure you burp them twice, or they will get gassy."

Lucien went back in and folded the cribs up and carried them to the van.

Landson Shaw settled next to him. "I'm so sorry things have come to this. I assure you they will get the best care."

"I know. You will make sure they thrive."

"Of course."

"You will send reports to Jordan on a regular basis."

"You're doing the best thing for them." Landson shook Lucien's hand. Lucien didn't wait for them to leave. He turned and went back inside the ranch to find his uncle.

Jordan sat on his leather chair in the lab. His eyes were peering into his microscope lens. The white lab coat he was wearing looked huge on his slight stature. For the first time, Lucien saw the aftermath of his heart attack.

"It's done." He leaned in close.

"I didn't hear you come in." Jordan paused what he was doing and took his glasses off. "It's for the best."

"If I hear someone say that again, I am going to crack, Uncle..."

"They mean no harm."

"How much time does she really have?"

"It's too hard to tell. If she keeps having seizures, it will continue to do harm. So far, her organs haven't shut down."

"What are you going to do about it?" Lucien sat down next to his uncle with inquisitive eyes.

"I have a temporary solution." He picked up a vial containing a pink substance and held it in the air.

"Temporary?"

"This will keep Samantha's and the baby's

immune systems fighting." He put vial down carefully.

"That's a start."

"Unfortunately. I wish it were more."

Lucien sighed inwardly and thought again about what Banth said to him at Dulce. "Are the other babies still healthy?"

"Landson said they are thriving and growing at a fast pace. He assured me they will be okay."

"What will happen to them?"

"They will be cared for and placed like all the hybrids."

"What if..."

"They may not even be Samantha's offspring. Doing a DNA test is foolish. It will only make her suffer more if it's positive. Put that thought out of your mind, son."

"Uncle, you say that with so much taciturnity in your voice. But—if they were ours. They are to live a life never knowing their parents, like me and my brothers and Eden."

"My boy, you don't even know for sure they are yours."

"I have no idea what they did to me while in the light."

"I am realistic."

"You're starting to sound like Eden." Lucien bit down hard on his tongue.

Michael came in the lab with Nathan Moore.

They both settled near Jordan. "You're back?" Jordan said.

"I have someone I want to introduce you to." Nathan opened his iPad. "I want you both to meet Dr. Jenter Ceria."

A thin man in a lab coat appeared on Nathan's iPad.

"Dr. Taylor, it's a pleasure to finally meet you. I wish it were under better circumstances."

Jordan nodded and moved closer to the screen on Nathan's iPad.

"After reviewing the lab reports and **MRI** and **CAT** scan on Samantha Hunter and her baby, there's something I need to tell you that may cure her. I feel it is an option, although not one you will like."

"Yes, yes, tell us! What are you waiting for, man?" Jordan said.

"It may work."

"Tell us," Jordan said.

"There are risks."

"Come on, man, spit it out!"

Michael and Nathan locked eyes. Their faces were grim.

"It's not Sam's alien blood causing the problem. Although it is compromising her immune system."

"Then what is it?" Lucien yelled out.

"It's a virus destroying her brain stem..."

"Banth's virus," Michael said.

A moment of silence.

"It's comparable to Brainstem Cavernous Angiomas. The virus is causing lesions on the brain stem. That's what's causing the seizures, in other words, blood from a hemorrhage is entering brain tissue, surrounding the cavernous angioma."

"Dear Lord," Jordan said, almost slumping over to sit.

"The only thing that may save her and the baby is a serum from Lucien's brain stem. His DNA has the healing properties against this alien virus."

"That's impossible," Nathan shouted.

"But... I couldn't heal them. I tried. Why would my brain stem serum work?"

"Your alien DNA has something in it that your sibling doesn't have. Maybe it's because your gift is to heal. That may cure her."

"May? That's a big may, Dr. Ceria," Nathan said.

"Well then, we have to try." Lucien stood.

"There has to be a better option," Nathan said.

"Let's do it," Lucien said with a breath.

"No! It can kill you," Eden said from the doorway.

"It's a possibility. You have to think of that, Lucien," Michael said. Daniel and Gabe left the room with heavy feet.

"Don't you know? I'm indestructible." Lucien gave her half a smile.

"In another life, maybe," Eden said.

"You have to make up your mind, Lucien. Sam and the baby don't have much time," Dr. Ceria said.

25 THE TEST

The morning sun's rays sneaked through the blinds and shone on Lucien's snowy diamond eyes. I remembered the night he stayed with me on the Sandia mountainside before we left Earth. I had never seen anything so beautiful. Everything that happened since then had led me to this point.

I was always dying. Like a cat with nine lives. I'd cheated death not once but many times. Fate's cheap joke. And the joke was on me.

Maybe I was supposed to die at Hidden Valley when my car plummeted over the embankment. I thought back to that day while I watched Lucien admiring little Ory in his crib.

* * *

"We're here." I struggled to get the words out. "Help!" I tried shouting, but the belt made it hard to raise my voice.

There was no way they would find us. Just when I thought all hope was lost, I felt someone at my side.

It was Lucien. I didn't know that then, but I see now it was him.

"Don't be afraid. I got you," he said, and he spoke gently to me, instantly soothing my worries as the seatbelt snapped open, and I could breathe again.

"She's free." His words rolled off his lips. I thought I was dead. And he was my angel. My beautiful angel. My fingers trailed loosely at my side as he dragged me across the dry soil. He laid me down on the forest ground away from the wreckage and pulled his shirt off and tucked it underneath my head. I was enveloped in his scent.

"My brother?" I whispered, my voice still not as strong as it should've been.

"Shhh. Don't try to speak," the stranger said, pushing my hair away from my face. When he did, a calmness swept over me.

* * *

Cassiel was right; he should have left me to die, and then none of this would be happening.

* * *

I lay still after another convulsion. I watched Lucien gaze at our son as he slept. My sweet son was suffering. And there was nothing I could do to ease his pain.

I finally broke the silence.

"How much more can he take?" My words were slow.

Lucien's trance was broken. "Not much more... I am so sorry."

I could tell by his expression he had something on his mind. I tried to read his thoughts. Nothing. All my alien superpowers were gone. I hadn't seen Finn since our first day back at the ranch. I wondered if I would ever see him again.

"When I was at Dulce, I saw Cassiel just like I saw Finn."

"You did?" He gave me half a smile.

"He helped me." I smiled.

"Sure, he did."

"Don't be facetious."

He didn't say anything.

"Why are you fidgeting?"

He settled near me, taking my hand. The worry on his face left him looking years older than he was.

"Sam...I have to talk to you. And before you answer, I am going to do it. I thought long and hard about it."

"By the look on your face, it's not good." I struggled to take a breath.

Lucien's eyelids dropped. I followed his gaze out the glass door at his family. I could see them sitting in the lab through the glass.

"You're right. It's bad, Sam..."

He didn't say anything. I could hear the clock

ticking; it was so loud because of the silence. "Delaying telling me isn't going to make it go away." I squeezed his hand tight.

He sighed. "Okay." He lowered his head a moment as if trying to get the courage to tell me. "You have a virus that is destroying...your brain stem." He paused and took a breath.

"Jordan fixed it. He's been giving me a serum."

"That's just a temporary fix, Sam. I wish it weren't."

"You can heal me like before. When the car went down the embankment and at the fair." He was silent. Tears welled in his eyes.

"Lucien... Lucien...what? Tell me."

"There's a cure. Well, sort of..."

"Why the hesitation? Why aren't we doing it?" I watched Ory gasp for air.

"There's just one tiny thing. And I have to tell you before we do it."

"Okay..."

"There's doctor from Division Six who thinks he can fix the problem."

"Then why the long face?"

He paused, clearing his throat. "Since my DNA can heal, and I don't get sick like humans, there is a chance the fluid in my brain stem can kill the virus that's causing lesions on your brain. And the baby."

"Lucien, what do you mean?"

"Surgery to extract my brain stem fluid."

"No..."

"There is no other choice, Sam." Lucien held his breath.

"The doctor said it was a piece of cake. I'll be fine."

"That's not even an option!" I took hold of his wrist.

"I'm doing it."

"No. I can't let you."

"Listen, it'll work. I just had to tell you how it was going to be done. Not for your approval."

"Is that our only option?"

"Yes."

"Why is this happening? I finally got you back."

"Jordan already has the lab being prepared. And the surgeon is being flown in as we speak."

"Lucien, this is so extreme." I felt myself losing control of my words. "...There ha-s-s—"

My body tensed up, and my body temperature soared. My limbs stiffened, and my head began to rock back and forth, and my arms went limp.

Lucien hurriedly held my arms down.

Jordan must have saw what was going on in the room through the glass. "She's seizing," I heard Lucien say.

"She's in the second stage."

Lucien and Jordan held me down until it passed.

Nathan brought a cold rag for my forehead. "She's not going to be able to come back from the next one. You know that, don't you?" He turned away and looked at Lucien.

My breathing quieted, and my temperature lowered.

"You okay?" Lucien said, moving my hair from my face and wiping my mouth. "You see why the operation has to be done?"

Jordan took my pulse.

"Dear Samantha, Ory will not survive a seizure like this. If Lucien doesn't do the operation, both of you will die," Jordan said.

I was weak, but I wasn't stupid. I knew there was no other way.

"I can't let you do this." More tears escaped my eyes and rolled down my cheek.

Lucien wiped them. "And I can't let you both die when I can save you."

Eden walked in and hovered over the baby. "Did you tell her?"

Lucien didn't speak through his words. I knew he thought it and Eden could read his mind.

"He's right, Sam. As much as I don't want to lose my brother, I don't want to lose Ory."

My gaze caught hers.

"Eden, no." Lucien said.

"What aren't you telling me?" I tried to sit up. "What?"

I watched Jordan's body stiffen. Lucien stood and raked his dark locks. "Tell me," I almost shouted.

Eden shook her head. "It doesn't matter."

"Yes, it does."

"He's sacrificing himself for you."

"That's enough!" Jordan bellowed so loud the baby screamed, and the rest of the Fosters heard.

"What's she talking about?" I said.

Michael stepped in. "In her rude, useless, immature way, she is saying Lucien will not survive the operation, or if he did, he would most likely be a vegetable."

The room became still like the eye of a hurricane.

"No!" I screamed. "I won't let you do it." I began to sob uncontrollably.

"Sammy, it's okay. I'll be fine. Look what you've done!" Lucien yelled back at his siblings.

"I can't let you do it!"

"I'll survive. I made it out of Area 51, didn't I?"

"Barely!"

Eden picked up the crying baby. Daniel and Gabe stormed out.

"You can't sacrifice your life... I won't let you."

"Sam, it's done."

I turned my head, weeping through more seizures.

26 JOE

"I want her father here if I don't make it out of surgery."

"I understand," Jordan said.

"I'm going to take off before she gets too sick."

"Everything will be ready for when you get back. I'll see to it."

"Text me if anything should happen while I'm gone."

"You do what you have to do, son." He hugged Lucien.

Lucien peeked in on Sam one last time with a heavy heart.

* * *

The New Mexico sun beaded down on Lucien's forehead as he stepped out of his Camaro. He looked up at the sky, wishing he didn't have to do this. He could feel his skin change from snowy white to a tawny, golden shade; it was a constant reminder as to where he came from.

Lucien could see Joe Hunter looking out his curtain and grimaced. He was on the front porch before Lucien made it to the walkway.

"You are here means only one thing," he said with his hands on his hips. The front door swung open and out came a tall, thin blonde woman with jeans and a plaid shirt.

"Lucien Foster, this is Kate, my wife."

She smiled and held out her hand. "Hello, Lucien, happy to meet you."

Lucien smiled with a firm shake. "How do you do?"

"We got hitched in Vegas. I tried telling Sammy, but every time I called, the voice mail picked up. After the odd call from Nathan Moore saying she was at your ranch, I figured she's still mad. Then your uncle called and told me she was being detained again by the NSA. I didn't know who to believe, so I stopped calling. She's eighteen—she can do what she likes, but I don't like it one bit."

"We need to talk, and I think it's best you come with me to the ranch alone."

"Why, what's going on at the ranch with Sammy?" He rushed to Lucien.

"You need to come to the ranch."

Dark clouds covered them with shade.

Joe paused a moment before punching Lucien in the jaw. Lucien was flung backward.

"Joe! Stop it, he's a kid." Kate ran to Lucien.

"Kid, my ass. Tell that to someone else."

"It's okay. He's right."

"I've been wanting to do that ever since you brought her home after keeping her out all night on Halloween!"

"What's gotten into you, Joe?" Kate said.

Lucien held his jaw. "Let him. If it makes him feel better. I wish I could punch myself." Black blood oozed from his lip.

"What the—" Joe walked up to Lucien's face. "What's that...on your lip?" He moved away, taking Kate's arm.

Lucien wiped his lip on the back of his hand.

"Come to the ranch with me, and I will explain."

"What are you, Foster?"

"Now you know why you have to come to the ranch."

"I always knew there was something off about you!"

"This is not open to debate. Please don't make me... Just get in your car."

"I am not going anywhere without the police."

"Joe, let's go in the house so I can clean up Lucien's face and the two of you can talk like adults." Lucien held his jaw.

"There is no need to discuss anything. I don't care what you are, or where you came from. All I care about is my daughter. We will follow you to your ranch. And then I am taking Sammy home. You understand?"

"I wish it were that easy. I truly do."

27 RUSSIAN SPY'S

Twilight began to fall on Highway 54. Streaks of colors splashed across the horizon. Any other time, Lucien would have found comfort watching the sunset. But tonight, he only saw pain and sorrow in the scenery. He glanced out the side window and took in the heavens. This might be the last night he would ever see it. He thought back on his life on Earth. He glanced at the rearview mirror at Joe's Navigator. He turned on the radio to play his CD of Beethoven's Moonlight Sonata. A rush of memories flooded his mind.

His uncle did everything he could to make him human growing up. He never questioned the existence of his maker. He knew there was something more to this world other than humans and aliens.

He struggled every day to do the right thing. Not a day went by that he didn't fight his alien urges, and there were many.

Sam changed all that. She was flawed just like he was. That was why he was drawn to her. They fit together like a puzzle. He had to be with her, he had to have her, to consume all of her. Was that the alien in him or something else he hadn't discovered yet?

Lucien thought of Gloria. He never got to know his mother. Memories of cradling her in his arms while she died overtook him. How he wished he could have gotten to know her. He recalled that moment while she took her last breath.

* * *

"How long did you know I was your son?" Lucien said while a tear streamed down Gloria's cheek.

"Long enough."

He looked into her gray eyes. The same as his. In the middle of chaos, Lucien held her tight.

"There's so much I need to ask you."

"You know all you need."

"We were on the capsule. With other beings."

"It doesn't matter now." She coughed.

"Were you there?" he said.

"I was their incubator, that is all."

"I don't understand." He tightened his grip while Gloria's life drained from her.

"Am I part human?"

She nodded. "They do what they do."

He remembered saying those exact words to Sam. "Is that yes?" Lucien bellowed.

"You are nothing like..."

"Like what?"

"You are good." She took something from beneath her gray smock and handed it to Lucien. He looked at the engraved symbols.

"Wait." He fumbled in his pocket. He pulled out the device he'd found in the artifact lab. It looked the same. "What is this? They look alike."

"It's a key to the truth, my son."

"What do you mean?"

"You are good."

"Tell me...Gloria!"

She smiled.

"Goodbye, my son." She closed her eyes.

"Sam, Lucien, this mountainside is going up and fast," Nathan Moore yelled.

"Leave me, Lucien," she said.

"I need to know."

Gloria smiled again while her eyes fixated on the sky above.

* * *

Lucien pressed his foot hard on the accelerator and looked in the rearview mirror at Joe's Navigator again. Joe would never forgive himself if Sam didn't make it, and Lucien would never forgive himself either. It would have all been for nothing, rescuing her in Hidden Valley. Thoughts of the accident flashed through his mind. All the times they shared. His thoughts once again drifted.

Lucien remembered when he altered time and

drove to Roswell Museum. Sam and he traipsed through the museum that resembled a movie theater. "UFO" edged in bold script and orange coloring printed vertically and horizontally on the building, and an image of a flying saucer. The checkerboard flooring. It all seemed like a dream. He chuckled to himself when he remembered the animated gray and white alien posed at the entrance.

He and Sam held hands as they walked. He smiled, thinking of Sam taking selfies with "Ralf," the oversized creature with a large head. They walked through each room with different themes. MJ 12, Project Blue Book. He remembered getting sad when he saw a metal sculpture of an alien figure. They walked through the history room with artifacts and antique ham radios. The montage of memories of them star-gazing. Watching It's a Wonderful Life on the couch. Joe putting Christmas lights up on the house. And when he went into the house to get more extension cords, Lucien used his telekinesis to put lights on the house. The look on Joe's face when he came out of the house, stunned, was priceless. He and Sam laughed as it began to snow.

A tear streamed down Lucien's face as he recalled Sam dancing in the snow, laughing. He wiped the tear away with the back of his hands. He thought for a moment when he was young just learning how to be human. Jordan was amazed when he cried his first tears. Jordan didn't know it was possible.

* * *

"Uncle, I watered it every day." Lucien held the dried-up fig tree in a red pot in his small hands.

"I see that, son." Jordan took the pot from his hands and placed it on his workbench.

"Why is it dying?"

He held his hands out, facing the tree, and light radiated from them. "Nothing. It's still dying."

"Lucien, there are some things in life we have no power over."

"But I heal; that is what I do. Gabe shapeshifts, and I heal."

"Not in this case, you don't. You must learn to accept what you cannot change. There will be some things you can't heal. Your heavenly father had other plans for this plant."

"My heavenly father does not like me."

"No, my boy, that is not why the fig tree is dying."

"Then what? I failed. I don't want the fig tree to die." Huge tears streamed down Lucien's boyish face.

Jordan bent down. "You are crying, my boy!" Jordan touched Lucien's face with his fingertips.

"Is that bad, Uncle?"

"No... Nooo, it is good!" He hugged Lucien.

"How is this possible? You're not human." Jordan rubbed his teary fingertips together.

"I don't want to be from the sky. I want to be human like you."

"Awe, Lucien. Don't let anything get you down. Especially that. That's the only way to live like a human. You have the heart of a human, and that's all that matters! That's all that matters."

* * *

He wiped another tear from his eye and raked his hand through his hair. Then his thoughts went to Sam. He wanted her from the very first moment their eyes met. Yes, it wasn't the alien in him; it was the human Jordan raised him to be.

He loved Sam. Aliens couldn't love; they just desired like animals. Jordan raised him to be human, but it had to be Gloria that made him human, he thought.

Gravel spit against the Camaro's tires as Lucien pulled into the driveway of the ranch. He edged closer to the garage doors.

Joe Hunter was right behind, parking close to the Camaro. Lucien got out first. The door slammed, and Joe and Kate followed Lucien up the driveway. They both were looking all around the ranch.

"Cameras?" Joe's gaze went to the surveillance camera following him. He motioned for Kate to go ahead of him.

"Now, why don't I feel this isn't unusual for you?

I should have known better than to let my daughter associate with you after the FBI came to my house! You were trouble from the start."

Lucien didn't answer.

"I can understand one camera, but...this is overkill. Now, this is weird."

He stood back and looked up at the roof.

"A red metal roof? Energy-efficient and check out that satellite attached to it. You need two satellites? And that one is not Direct TV— like to see the smarts behind that."

"And you will."

"You guys Russian Spy's?"

He looked at the property beyond the barn. "A telescope that big out here."

Joe stopped, turned around, and scanned the front and side of the ranch. "More cameras. Okay, you're out in nowhere land, and you need these many cameras."

"Joe..." Kate took hold of Joe's arm. "Stop."

Lucien shrugged it off and walked up to the front door.

He didn't use his key. He waved his hand right in front of Joe.

Joe grimaced and stepped back. "What is that? Some sort of magic trick?" Lucien didn't answer. "I knew it! You're one of those mechanically engineered humans the government cooked up! There had to be more to you than meets the eye.

And with that crazy high IQ."

Lucien grimaced. "Not exactly... Why didn't you ever say anything? If you had your suspicions?"

"Who would have believed me? If I had gone to the authorities, they would have said I was another easterner kook that moved to Roswell."

"You should have said something."

"It would have made my life a hell of a lot easier. Sam with her crazy conspiracy theories. She was right on it, huh?"

"When did you figure it out?"

"Not until I just saw you do that with your hand. I had my suspicions when I couldn't find anything on you when I did a background check. Not even a driver's license and birth records at the college or courthouse."

Lucien closed the door behind them.

"I'm going to take you somewhere, and you can never say it exists, and that includes your new wife."

"Why? Will you kill if me if I do?"

Lucien did not smile or chuckle.

"You're serious?"

"Not me. But others would."

Joe didn't smile either.

"Do you understand?"

"I do."

Lucien didn't want to do any mind control on him this time. He wanted Joe able to see his daughter and be there for her if he did not make it out of the surgery.

He lifted the tapestry hiding the secret elevator. "No one."

Joe and Kate nodded.

Joe didn't move. But Lucien could tell by his expression he was intrigued.

Lucien gestured for Kate and Joe to get into the elevator. Joe was reluctant at first. He stepped in. Kate gazed at Lucien a moment until Lucien held out his arm for her to go first. He stepped inside.

"I hope I'm not going to regret this," Joe said.

"I think it's a little too late for that."

Lucien hit the down button, and the elevator door closed. There was apprehension in Joe's eyes. "Wait! Promise me you're not a Russian Spy."

"I'm not a spy."

The elevator door shut and down they went fast. Joe gave a half-smile and held on.

"Dear Lord, don't let him be a spy!"

The door opened to the underground dwelling the Fosters called home. The lights shone a low bluish light against the marble and crystal hallway.

"Whoa, look at this place."

The usual humming of the water filters. Classical music played. Lucien led Joe to the conference room within a glass enclosure. "Follow me."

At first, Joe's feet seemed to be glued to the floor. Lucien went first. Joe and Kate followed nervously. "It's okay," Lucien said, gesturing for them to sit.

They stood where Jordan, Taylor, Dr. Jenter Ceria, Daniel, Gabe, Michael, and Nathan Moore were seated.

Joe immediately locked eyes with Nathan. A heavy, uneasy presence filled the room. "What the hell are you doing here?" Joe sprang in Nathan Moore's face.

"Calm down, Mr. Hunter. We'll explain!"

Kate took Joe's arm. "Joe."

Lucien could tell it was not going to be easy telling Sam's father that Nathan Moore had been involved with the Fosters all along. Joe was intelligent and knew something was going on from the start.

"Nathan? What's going on? Out with it!" Joe stepped forward.

"Joe, take it easy. We will explain everything. You have to relax."

"Relax? You people have been nothing but trouble to my daughter, and it's going to stop here."

He took his phone from his pocket.

"I wouldn't do that if I were you," Gabe said.

"I don't scare easily."

Michael waved his hand, and Joe's phone went flying around the room. Joe ducked, taking Kate with him as he ran to the door.

"You have no idea who you are messing with, and if I were you, I would sit down and listen," Gabe said.

"I think I have a pretty good idea."

"Joe, just listen to them. Please," Kate pleaded with him. Lucien pulled up a chair for Joe and Kate.

"Sit," Lucien said.

"Nephew. Be kind."

"The Fosters are extraterrestrial biological entities, EBEs for short," Nathan said calmly but firmly.

"So, you're telling me when we went on that dig in Dulce, you knew that Lucien was an EBE?"

"Yes, Joe. I was working with Division Six."

"Division Six?"

"A group of scientists and government officials who broke away from the government and formed Division Six to protect the Fosters," Jordan said politely.

"Why couldn't you just be spy's."

Joe took Kate's hand and bolted to the door.

Lucien raised his hand, slamming the door shut in front of Joe's face. "Seriously, man, where do you think you're going to go?"

Joe reached for his phone on the ground. "I'm calling the FBI; DOD I don't care!"

"They can't help you because they are part of the equation," Nathan said.

Lucien waved his hand. This time, his phone went flying with such force, it smashed against the wall.

"The reason we brought you here is because

Sam and your grandson are dying," Nathan said.

Joe's face went pale. "My what?"

"We have just enough time to save them. My nephew is the only one who can save the baby and Samantha," Jordan said.

"What are you talking about?"

"Maybe if you would listen instead of fighting us," Gabe said.

Lucien was quiet. His mind was on Sam and the baby.

"We brought you here because there's a possibility all three will perish."

"Sam is dying," Joe said. "What did you do to her?" His hands were reaching for a chair. Kate hurried and got the chair for him to sit.

Michael helped Joe to the chair, and suddenly, Joe was sitting trembling.

"What do you have to do?" He spoke in a monotone voice. All the anger was gone; in its place were fear and disbelief.

"First, you're going to pull yourself together, then you are going to meet your grandson and reunite with your daughter," Michael said.

Joe rubbed his brow and nodded.

28 WE DIE ANYWAYS

"Why is it every time you are with him you end up in a hospital bed?"

I slowly turned my head. "Daddy?" I said through a haze taking my vision. I wanted to sit up, but I was too weak. Before I knew it, my father was sitting near me. He took my hand and lightly squeezed it.

"Every time," my dad said with a raspy voice.

"That's not true, and you know it."

I struggled to smile.

My words slurred when I spoke. But I knew he would be able to hear me. He pushed my damp hair from my face.

"Sammy..."

I couldn't believe those words were coming from him. I thought I'd never hear his voice again. I tried to sit up.

"No, don't. Lie there and rest."

"Daddy."

"Sammy, what have they done to you?"

"No one did this." I wanted to close my eyes.

"What happened to you?"

"You see your grandson? You see him…"

My dad got up and went to the cradle.

"My little Ory…he's on a ventilator."

I hated seeing my dad like this. His hands trembled.

"How's any of this possible? When did this happen?"

I smiled. "I thought they told you."

"They did, but, it's crazy."

"You…of…all people should know it's possible. You're a scientist."

"I'm an archeologist; this science doesn't have anything to do with it."

"That's not true. You studied ancient civilizations."

"Yes, I know that the Sumerians, ancient Mayans, and Egyptians all believed in space travel, but I never actually believed in it. I just thought the Roswell crash was a hoax."

I chuckled inwardly. "He's…"

"He's trouble. Just like I said before. That hasn't changed."

"This isn't his fault." I grabbed the bed rail. "It's not."

By my father's expression, I knew he didn't believe me. I took a breath.

"They said you have changed into something like them."

"Not anymore. My alien side is dying from this virus."

"How many viruses are there?"

"There are many. Too many to count."

"Is this the same one that's an epidemic now?"

"No...this is entirely different. You can't catch this. But, Dad, there is one that is killing humans. You have to take precautions."

"I wasn't worried about that, honey."

"I know you weren't, but the other I'm talking about can kill you in minutes."

"The news said it's under control. They made a vaccine. I am worried about you. Nothing more."

"I'm going to be fine. But the viruses keep mutating, and the vaccines can't keep up." I tried to smile.

"Lucien will fix this?" my dad said, pulling up the chair to sit near me. I turned my head. Tears welled in my eyes.

"I don't want him to. It will kill him."

"Sam, he owes it to you."

"No, he doesn't, Daddy." I looked in his eyes. "Lucien is a special gift from the heavens. To lose such a magnificent creature is a sin."

"Let him do it. They brought me here to convince you."

"I don't mind dying. I will see Finn and Mom again."

"Do it for my grandson."

"What if he does it and we die anyway?"

"At least he tried."

"I don't want him to do it."

"Sam, he's doing it anyway. He just wanted your blessing." The door opened. Lucien stood with a solemn expression.

My father stood and kissed my cheek. I took his hand, not wanting to let it go.

Lucien watched him leave. He stood a moment, not saying a word. He crept to the cradle and took Ory's hand.

Little Ory wrapped his hand around Lucien's finger. "Do you remember Sandia Mountainside?"

"How could I forget?"

"I said I would love you forever." He turned with tears.

"Don't say another word."

"I'm not going to say anything else. I just came to tell you they are ready for me."

"And what am I supposed to tell your son someday if you die?" My chin quivered, and my chest rose with each breath as I began to sob.

Lucien clenched tearfully. "The same thing I told you. Tell him to live his life. To endure middle school, high school. Go to the mall, work out, hang out with his friends. Be a normal kid and someday he'll find the love of his life."

Tears rolled down my face as he spoke.

"You'll tell him just like I told you on the

mountainside when I thought I'd never see you again. Tell him his dad loved him. Forever. I love you, Sam."

He opened the door and paused, gazing at me. I could almost hear his heartbeat. He started to leave.

"Lucien... Always and forever."

"Forever."

29 ANOTHER TEST

"Damn, you're killing my arm."

"Seventy-two over sixty-eight. Does your race run a normal low?" Dr. Jenter Ceria said.

"I don't know...My brothers and sister run a low like me," Lucien said, rubbing his arm where the cuff was.

"Interesting."

Jordan brought in a high mechanical surgical tool. "This will do most of the procedure," Jordan said.

Both men were dressed in scrubs. Lucien lay in the hospital lab near Sam. Classical music played. He could see Eden crying in the other room through the glass.

"Someone please tell her I am going to be okay. My body will kick into survival mode."

Michael and Gabe were silently pacing the floor. He could tell this was tearing them apart, but he knew this had to be done. He gazed at Daniel working on the computers. Joe Hunter and Kate sat with Sam, consoling her.

There was a surreal feeling all around Lucien. He took heavy breaths and squeezed his hands open and closed as Jordan shut the drapes to begin the procedure.

"You are sure you want to do this?" Jordan said.

Lucien nodded.

Jordan took his arm and started an IV.

"I have to, Uncle."

Jordan grimaced. "I know you do. I am going give you something to calm you before we start?"

"No... I'm fine."

"You sure?"

"Yes, just get on with it."

"I will be assisting Dr. Ceria. I'll be here the whole time."

Lucien nodded.

Jordan went to place the anesthesia mask on Lucien's face. Dr. Ceria pushed a surgical tray close to Lucien.

They raised the music. Lucien closed his eyes in anticipation just when the door burst open. "Wait!" Daniel and Nathan Moore Daniel rushed in.

Lucien sat up.

"We have a visitor. Dejaha Zoris."

"Zoris?" Jordan dropped the mask.

"Get him out of here before I rip him limb to limb!" Lucien yelled.

A moment passed. Nathan brought Dejaha Zoris in with Michael. His tall stature dwarfed even the

Fosters. His shaved head glistened from the bright surgical lights.

"He's a traitor. He chained me to a wall! He's the reason Sam is dying."

"Lucien, you don't understand. I had to play along with Banth's charade!"

"I don't believe him! Uncle, get him out of here."

"There's a cure! On Moira," Zoris said.

"You told me there is no Moira, Zoris!"

Zoris was a dead man by the way Jordan held his gaze.

"I tell you, there's a cure!"

"Lucien, he is telling the truth," Nathan said.

"Are you?" Jordan said.

Zoris nodded.

Hope filled Lucien's heart. He started to remove the blood pressure cuff and ripped out the IV and stood.

"The girl and the baby can survive on Moira. They have an antidote. It works on the T cells."

"We can't get them there."

Lucien's hopes came crashing down.

Daniel approached them. "Yes, we can. There is a portal."

"The equinox has gone and went," said Lucien.

"Not talking about an equinox—that's a window."

"We call them X-points or electron diffusion regions," explained Dejaha Zoris.

"Yes, Nasa was researching this with Nikola

Tesla before he died in nineteen forty-three. We tried searching for his research, but the government confiscated it. He said beings from outer space gave him the information telepathically. It's a wireless-powered worldwide energy source," Jordan said.

"There are places where the magnetic field of Earth connects to the magnetic field of the Sun, creating an uninterrupted path leading from our own planet to the sun's atmosphere ninety-three million miles away."

"They found it. Flux transfer event or 'FTE,'" said Nathan Moore.

"Ten years ago, I was pretty sure they didn't exist, but now the evidence is incontrovertible," Jordan said.

"We have used them for centuries," said Zoris.

"Why didn't I know about this?"

He ignored Jordan.

"They open and close several times a day," Zoris said.

"They're in space," Jordan said.

"How would we get Sam and the baby in space?"

"The sun is a stargate to Earth. The portal will open and close very quickly. It shines on the Earth, opening as a ray of light at the entrance to the portal."

"When is the next one?" Lucien said.

"We have no idea when," Dejaha Zoris said.

"Gentlemen! Why're we even thinking of portals

in space when we have one on Earth?" Jordan bellowed.

"Oh course..." Dejaha Zoris raised an eyebrow.

"London," Michael said.

"The oldest stargate is Stonehenge," Daniel said, looking right at his brother Lucien. "We need the key."

"Wait." Lucien had a look of realization. He ran over to his jeans that were folded on the chair, reached into his pocket, and pulled out the alien device from the artifacts lab. "I found this in Dulce. It's some kind of key by the look of it." The others stared in awe. Jordan took it. Lucien didn't show him the part that Gloria gave him.

"Where did you get this?" Jordan turned the device over and glided his fingers over the engraved symbols.

Joe's an archeologist he should look at this," Lucien said.

They left the surgical room and gathered in Jordan's library.

* * *

"These inscriptions are from the Hopi tribe for sure. They believe they can communicate with the Star-people," Joe said. "Where did you get this?"

"Dulce's artifacts lab," Lucien said.

"Nathan, we never saw anything like this when we're there," Joe said.

Nathan went to Jordan and looked at the item.

"Is this the missing data from the pod's log on the ship in Roswell?"

"It could be. We don't know for sure," Jordan said.

"Ok wait, wait this is my cue to exit. I'm going back to sit with Sammy. I'm not ready to hear about pods, and ships and missing data," Joe said leaving the library.

"If that's the case all these years, they've been telling the Division that it was lost, and they've just been keeping it right here?" Michael said.

"No...it was stolen by Banth. They would have never kept it from us," Daniel said.

"Finally! I can't believe you found this," Jordan said.

"Yes! Try to get a signal to Moira! This device will open the portal. It has to." Daniel raced to the communications room.

Lucien started to laugh.

"Yes, my boy, you can relax," Jordan said.

"You better get dressed. You got a trip to plan," Michael said.

"I have to tell Sam," Lucien said.

* * *

"Sam! Great news." Lucien said, gently touching her hand. He settled near her bedside. Jordan and the Fosters were watching in the distance from behind the glass enclosure. Jordan turned to leave the room, and the Fosters followed.

"You're going to be all right."

"You didn't have the surgery," Sam said. Her eyes were half closed.

Lucien pushed her hair back from her face. "You remember Dejaha Zoris? He's here. He's contacted, Moira. They have an antidote."

"But how will we get it?"

"That's why I am here. Zoris said we must go there. There's a portal. A stargate in Earth's electromagnetic field. We can't space travel...but there's a portal. When I was at Dulce, I found the missing data from our ship's log in Banth's artifacts lab. But this is what confuses me." He took the device from his pocket. "Jordan has the other one. Gloria handed me this before we left her. I'm not sure they go together yet. But I think they do. Look at the symbols."

"What do you think this one means?"

Lucien shrugged. "Not sure. Gloria wanted me to have it."

"You kept it from Jordan. Why?"

"All these years, Division has been telling us the that it was lost, and they've just been keeping it right here on Earth. It contains a key to a portal where we can step into and take us to Moira without space travel. If it's that simple, why would they keep it from us? Or better yet, why would they want us to stay on Earth? It doesn't make sense."

"That's wonderful. Why are you overthinking

this? They can save Ory and me."

"You're right. I'm overthinking. That's the plan, then, to get you well." Lucien smiled.

"When do we go?"

"Soon...only...one thing." His face got bleak.

"What aren't you telling me?"

"You can never come back."

30 PIECES OF GLASS

Lucien rubbed the key between his fingers. He left Sam to ponder what was happening. He put the key in his pocket and went to find the others.

They were in the communications room gathered around their computers. Jordan was seated in his black leather chair smoking a pipe. Michael, Gabe, and Daniel spoke among themselves. Eden had headphones on and was looking at a map of Earth on a massive computer screen.

Jordan gazed at Lucien.

Lucien's attention was on Eden's screen.

"How did she take it?" Jordan asked.

Lucien's eyes didn't leave the screen. "Well enough." He turned to Jordan.

"It will be okay," Jordan said.

"Where's Joe?" Lucien asked.

"I put him up in a hotel."

Lucien nodded. "That's good."

"They can say their last goodbyes as soon as the serum kicks in. I made it stronger. Sam will be well enough to travel."

"Jordan."

"You have something on your mind, son. What is it?"

"I can't stop thinking about something that Banth told me at Dulce," Lucien said.

"I wouldn't waste a second on anything he said," Michael said.

"And what about Zoris? I don't believe it was all hogwash. He seemed very convincing."

"You seem to want to discuss it. Out with it," Jordan said, taking a puff of his pipe.

"We have to celebrate! Brandy for you, Uncle," Eden said, standing.

He nodded and smiled. "Get one for your brother too."

"Banth said I am not from Moira, but an interdimensional palace. Where the light himself threw his finest. What does it mean?"

Jordan and Michael locked eyes with each other. "Just blabber from a lunatic," Michael said.

"Did he say anything else?" Jordan asked.

"Yes, ...he said I was from the kingdom of the serpent."

The piercing sound of glass smashing into a thousand shattered fragments onto the ceramic floor interrupted their conversation leaving an icy chill.

"Eden, you ok?" Michael hurried to help her.

"Be careful not to cut yourself, my dear," Jordan

said.

"Your brandy uncle. I'm so sorry."

Her hand trembled. She kept her gaze on Michael. His stare was just as intense. "What's with you," he whispered.

"I'm so clumsy," Eden said while she quickly picked up the broken pieces of glass.

"What were you saying," Jordan took his eyes off the shattered glass.

"The serpent. What do you think he meant by that?" Lucien's eyes glazed with anticipation.

"Your ancestors were Reptilian. Banth was poisoning your mind, son."

Lucien studied their faces. "Was he?"

"Son, Banth only cared about Samantha's DNA in the hope of creating some sort of super soldier alien. He had devious plans for yours and her offspring."

"Do you really believe that?"

"It's Banth, yes," Michael said.

"I have been thinking about that. Why?"

"You know why, Lucien. Because Samantha's blood mixed with yours. He wanted to create a super being."

"Something's not right. I can feel it in my bones."

"You're exhausted, and your mind is playing tricks on you."

"Is it?"

No one said anything.

"I didn't think so."

Lucien almost knocked over the chair and left the area.

"Lucien, where are you going?"

"I have some unfinished business I have to take care of."

31 THE KEY

Lucien couldn't think of anything else except for what Banth had said.

His words echoed in his mind and ate at him like a cancerous tumor. He left his family to be alone and to think.

He had an overwhelming feeling Jordan wasn't honest with him. He decided to take it upon himself to find the answers he was looking for.

He made sure no one was following him when he slowly opened Jordan's sleeping quarters and went to his desk.

He glanced at the door before he lifted the handle of the desk drawer, looking for the device he found at the artifacts lab in Dulce—the twin to the key-like device Gloria had given him. He rummaged through the drawer, then another, and another. Where is it? He thought to himself.

And there it was next to the crystal skull. Jordan had it sitting on a pedestal. He picked it up, looking at it carefully and reached into his pocket and took out the one Gloria had given him. He let his hand glide over the Hopi Indian engraved symbols. He turned it upside down, looking at the groove at the bottom, and then he looked at the other piece. It was like a puzzle; they fit perfectly together. He put them together, snapping them in place. The alien device lit up, a glow of different colors shining through the engraved symbols. He hurriedly pulled them apart. He looked in the direction of the door. Thankfully, no one saw the bright lights the device emitted. Whatever this was, he was keeping it to himself. He rushed out of Jordan's room.

What did this have to do with Moira? He kept hearing Gloria's voice in his head. "It's a key to the truth, my son."

Would anything change after going to Moira? And what if Moira was not what he thought it was? His feet led the way. He paused before stepping into the elevator when he noticed his crystal around his neck was glowing. The closer the device got to his crystal, the more it glowed. They seemed to be connected somehow. He took the strange key Gloria gave him and his crystal and went to search for its meaning.

He went as far down as he could go to a special storage area of the underground dwelling where Jordan kept his files. He couldn't shake the feeling that something wasn't right. The only one who ever came down here was Jordan. It was off limits to him and his siblings. What was Jordan hiding?

Lucien came upon the entrance. In front of him stood a circular structure. In the middle was a door resembling an old bank vault. His hands searched the door. A key code lock? Why would Jordan keep this locked he thought? He stepped back, gazing at the structure.

He meditated a moment to try to get inside Jordan's head. For a fleeting moment, Lucien felt guilty for doubting the only father figure he had. He closed his eyes and meditated again. He pictured Jordan. He entered his private thoughts, becoming one with his soul. The only problem—Jordan knew his abilities. All his siblings had the gift of telepathy, and Jordan knew how to block them.

Since Jordan knew how to keep his thoughts private, Lucien had to concentrate to get into his mind. He closed his eyes and placed his hands on the cold metal door. This drained Lucien, breaking the barrier of Jordan's secrets. Sweat beaded on his brow. His hands began to tremble until an image of a woman came into view. She was beautiful. His wife who died many years ago. Her birthday. 07, 25, 34. Lucien punched the numbers in and the safe popped open. He took a moment to compose himself before he walked into Jordan's private space.

He stared into the vault first before entering. Surprisingly, antique green lamps were on, emitting a soft glow from the inside of the vault.

He cautiously stepped in.

The safe was lined with news clippings and bookshelves that went as high as the ceiling. Hundreds of logs. Antique chairs and fixtures, and a century-old taupe loveseat in gold trim with red buttons filled the enclosure. The safe on the outside was deceiving. The depth of the secret chamber was larger than what he anticipated. Lucien stepped back, amazed. All this time, hidden inside the walls were scrolls. In the center of the room was a wooden table was a light, a chair, and an opened journal. Lucien flipped through the pages of the journal.

They were up to date. Jordan had still been writing in them. Since the lights were on, Lucien figured Jordan must have left in a rush and forgot to turn them off.

Lucien slowly made his way to the logs that were opened on vintage writing tables. He let his fingers glide, barely touching the scrolls. He suddenly began to flip through each of them, reading the dusty labels. The dates went as far back to the 1200s. He rubbed his brow. 1278, the 1400s?

Lucien took the log from 1947 out and brought it over to the table. He sat down, leaping through the pages. There were diagrams, physics problems, sketches, and notes on the String Theory. Nothing on Moira. Nothing. There were images of folklore ghosts, Nephilim, and Watchers! Like at Dulce. He closed it slowly and walked further, scanning the illuminated paintings on the dark walls.

One the walls were paintings from the Renaissance. The Annunciation by Carlo Crivell, The Madonna With Saint Giovannino, and The Crucifixion, a 14th-century painting in the Visoki Decani Monastery in Kosovo, which included human figures inside images of spacecrafts. The painting of The Madonna With Saint Giovannino included a figure in the background staring at the sky. The object the figure was looking at was a winged angel emanating light. There were religious paintings depicting UFOs in pictures going back to the 1400s.

Lucien was pondering the paintings when he came upon a small chest high on the corner bookshelf, too high for him to reach. He scanned the area. In the corner stood a six-step safety ladder. He carried it to the spot under the shelf with the chest and ascended the ladder carefully.

Jordan had secrets that needed to be told.

He lifted the chest carefully, climbed down the ladder, and set it on the table. He was surprised it had a lock as well. Lucien gazed at the door a moment. A twinge of guilt stung his conscience for wanting to invade Jordan's personal belongings. He took the key Gloria had given him from his pocket and looked at it for a moment. Maybe there was more to this key than the portal in London? He put the device from the artifacts lab and Gloria's key together, snapping them in place. The objects glowed but nothing else. He slowly put the key in the lock. Nothing. Then he noticed another groove at the top.

"Hmmm." He stared out into the strange room. He saw a row of crystal skulls radiating white light. He cocked his head. Then he looked down at the crystal around his neck. It suddenly hit him. He quickly lifted the crystal over his head and held it in his hand a moment, thinking. He took the end of the crystal and put it in the groove. Like a kaleidoscope, every color on the color wheel danced about the room, reflecting off Lucien's face. He stood back. When he did, a black box mechanically popped up with a ray of white light shining from it. Two sides of the box opened and a red-lined interior with an aged letter was revealed.

Lucien's eyes shot to the door, fearful Jordan would enter and find him intruding in his personal belongings. His hands moved slowly, reaching for the letter, which glowed a reddish orange seal. No return address. The print was sketchy and worn. He took the tattered letter with the wax broken seal dated 1947. His hands shook as he took the letter from the envelope and read its contents.

August 23,1947
Dear Jordan,
You must bring the infant named Lucien back to Wright-Patterson Air Force Base and go to Hangar 18 as soon as you read this. There s not much time. The other scientists

were murdered at Area 52, and you will be next
if you don t follow my instructions carefully.
It s not what you think you have. Jordan, it s
so much worse. We were all fooled. They want
to protect and hide their real identity. Every
one of us is in danger. If the baby is not
returned by midnight, the oracle will close.
The Illuminati are in control now. The host
was released into our atmosphere by the Black
Knight that has been orbiting our solar
system for thousands of years. There was
never a UFO that crash-landed in July. What
you have is the offspring of an
interdimensional being, and per the Bible, the
satanic offspring of the Fallen.

Do you know what you have? Jordan, Hurry!

Regards,
Lt. Col. Richard French.

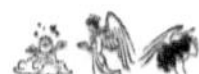

Lucien dropped the letter. "The offspring of the fallen?" His hands trembled.

He started to breathe heavily. The room began to shake. The books fell from the shelves and papers went flying like someone had turned on a fan.

Lucien bellowed.

Jordan rushed into the vaulted room.

"You lied to me, all of you. The Black Knight brought me here," Lucien said out loud.

"Lucien, calm yourself down."

"It wasn't a saucer from another word that crash-landed in Roswell in 1947."

"It was from another world."

"Yeah, right! What else have you lied about?"

"I didn't lie. I hid the truth to protect you."

"Call it what you want. You deceived me! Do the others know?" Lucien yelled, shaking the bookshelves. "Who are they to me?"

"You were never supposed to find out this way."

"When did you plan on telling me? When I went through the portal. Or is that a lie too?"

"The portal is true."

Lucien took a breath. "The satellite that has been orbiting the Earth for centuries brought me here; that's what Banth said. This letter proved it, and you have been hiding it. I am not some special being from somewhere in the universe!"

"Lucien, but you are," Jordan said.

"Don't 'Lucien' me! My blood is black for a reason. The light doesn't shine in my veins!"

"Your brothers and sister have the same blood."

"So, they are the same dark creatures?"

"Calm down and listen to me!"

"Stop with the lies!"

"I can't reason with you when you're like this."

"There never was Moira. You made that up too!" Lucien clenched his jaw.

"Moira is real," Jordan insisted.

"You're lying."

"I tried to protect you."

He stepped closer.

"I'm warning you, old man, to stand back!"

The wind picked up in the vault. Papers whipped by their heads. Jordan braced himself on his cane. He stumbled and fell to the ground. Books were thrown along with the tumbling of Jordan's antiques.

The last book fell. Lucien brought his hands to his sides and took a breath.

"Are you done with your temper tantrum?"

"The Black Knight is a beacon to my maker?"

They were both quiet.

"Who am I?" Lucien bellowed.

"You are you!"

"Stop with the riddles, Uncle!"

"What I can tell you is there are the Gray Skins, Reptilian, Norics, and other EBE. What I can't tell you is if they're from outer space. Before Lt. Col. French sent me that letter, I thought you were from the crash in Roswell. Everyone who saw the debris was taken and mysteriously disappeared. I never saw the remains. They wanted us to believe that it was a flying saucer and then they told the media it was a weather balloon. The other two creatures in the pod that was released by Black Knights were destroyed. They were the guardians of what was contained in the pod. They were living, breathing creatures, yes, like the No Whites are. They were alien, yes—in a way they were, but were they from outer space? The capsule that contained your DNA was taken to Dulce. I believe that is where Gloria comes in. And I don't need to tell you what they did at Dulce. One of the other scientist who was later killed sought refuge with me. She begged me to take care of you. She rescued you from Dulce and brought you to me. I made a vow to her I would protect you. A few years later in a dream, an angel came to me and told me I would get five visitors from a faraway land called Moira. Those visitors were your siblings. They found me and said they would protect you with their lives. What I can tell you is there are angels, fallen angels, and Watchers from another plane— in a different world, and that plane has been opened for almost a hundred years."

"Banth said I am one of the fallen like him."

Jordan helped himself up walked up to Lucien, looking him straight in the eye. "You are an interdimensional being. If you want to believe Banth, so be it."

"You don't deny it."

"Lucien, you are special. That's really all you need to know."

Lucien could feel another presence in the room.

"What's all the commotion?" Michael said, walking into the vault. Behind him were the rest of Lucien's siblings.

Lucien turned around.

They gathered around him and Jordan.

"What are you doing here, Lucien?" Michael said, looking at Jordan.

"He found the letter," Jordan said.

"You know what's in this! What it says," Lucien said.

"I do," Michael said.

"Who are you? You're not my brothers and sister. I was the only one brought here!" He gazed at them.

Michael held out his hand, and the letter found his palm. "We were protecting you, Brother," Daniel said.

"You're not my brother."

"I am."

"What were you protecting me from? Tell me!"

"Yourself."

Lucien took a breath and glared at Michael. "Don't play games with me."

"You are the fallen one. The offspring of an angel and human. A Nephilim," Michael said.

"Why the charade?" Lucien asked.

"We were protecting you from the others as well."

"The 'originals'?"

"They are angels like yourself," Daniel said.

"What kind of angels? They look nothing like the angels I've seen. I don't look like them." Lucien said.

"Of course, you wouldn't," Michael said.

"Because you were His most beloved one!" Eden said, stepping over a fallen lamp. She bent and picked up a scroll. She closed it and placed it on the table.

"What angel?" Lucien said. They were quiet a moment.

"Just tell him," Daniel said.

Gabe interrupted. "Lucien, we are here to protect you from a far more dangerous entity than you can image. Yourself. Who you were and are."

"You are the reincarnation of the Morning Star, Brother," Michael said, walking to Lucien.

"It's true." Lucien felt like the wind was knocked from him. He staggered back, bumping into Eden.

The room felt like it was swallowing him up.

"Can't you see this is too much for him?" Eden tried to comfort him.

"What else?"

Daniel was the next to speak. "I am the seventh of the twenty Watchers. The leader of the two hundred fallen angels. I taught the signs of the sun to humans. I communicate with the interdomains and the elementals."

Daniel stepped aside, and Michael stepped forward.

"I am the archangel Michael who battled wicked angels and waged war with our father."

"My father?"

"Tell him the truth," said Gabe.

Eden took Lucien's hand. "Do not be angry, or fear us, Brother. My true name is Uriel; I was once the angel left on Earth to stand guard at the gates of Eden."

Lucien pulled his hand away as his eyes welled with unshed tears. Gabe stepped forward.

A tear broke free from Lucien's eyes. "Let me guess."

"Archangel Gabriel." His eyes glowed with a warm yellow-white light. Lucien could feel the warmth and love flow from them into his heart.

"You..."

Gabe gave Lucien a half smile. "The messenger angel, acting as a messenger of our Father." "Your father, Lucien. Our father."

"I don't understand. If I am who you say I am, why don't I have any memory?"

"Because our father had me cast you down to Earth for eternity in your first life. Your memory was taken as punishment, and your wings were clipped if you didn't know who you were what harm could you do. You were supposed to be kept underground."

"Dulce?"

"Yes..."

"I don't get it. The president? Banth, O'Neil, Raul Roman?"

"Your dark force minions."

"But how—"

"You were cast out and now reborn, but your son is the prince."

The room beamed a bright light. They shielded their eyes.

"Cassiel," Eden said, rushing in his direction, hugging him.

Cassiel's light lit up the vault. "You're dead," Lucien said.

"Angels can die, but we can be reborn."

"You hated Sam. You didn't want me to save her."

"I was protecting her not you. I wanted to prevent the prophecy."

White, glistening wings spread the length of the room. A single feather blew in front of Lucien.

"Cassiel is the angel of solitude and tears," Eden said.

Cassiel's wings retracted and disappeared.

"The speed of God." Michael hugged his brother.

"We are all archangels, not aliens, Brother," Michael said.

"There are more archangels," Cassiel added.

"Where are they, then?" Lucien said.

Another light shined lighting up the entrance of the vault. It was Nathan Moore.

"We take on all forms," Nathan said.

"AKA Rafael the supreme healer," Gabe said with a chuckle.

"Why can I heal?"

"Because your healing came from your wings and when Michael clipped them that power should have left you, but it didn't. The power went through your body and out of your hands. We all have special gifts just like you always thought. Some of us more than others."

"If you can heal more than I why can't you heal Sam?"

"It's not His plan."

Lucien grimaced and backed away from them. "I don't believe any of you."

"Son, I know it's a lot to take in. And none of it makes sense why we did what we did. We were protecting you from Banth and the other Watchers," Jordan said.

"All those aliens and hybrids at Dulce?"

"They are Cambions— demon and human offspring's."

Lucien looked at Daniel and grimaced. "You are a Watcher?"

"I was supposed to watch over them on Earth. I broke free from them. What they were doing was against nature," Daniel said. He continued

"When it all started there was a war on Moira."

"Michael and his angels fought against our father's favorite and his dark angels fought back. But he was not strong enough, and they lost their place in Moria. He was hurled down—that ancient serpent called Lucifer, who led the whole world astray. He was hurled to Earth underground, and his angels with him," Cassiel said.

"You, Lucien," Eden said. "We tweaked your name. The other just didn't seem like a good idea." Eden tried to smile.

"In 1947, when Banth saw that you had been hurled back to Earth again, he pursued you. And when the young scientist snuck you out of Dulce. You were safe for a while. But then as you grew up things changed like Samantha. The 'No Whites' found you and Sam. And when you two were taken back into the false light of the Black Knight the day of the Christmas Solstice...It was too late." Gabe said.

"And giving birth to the male child, Sam was given two feathers of your wings. That was your DNA so that she might fly to the place prepared for her in the desert, where she would be taken care of for a time," Daniel continued.

"You call that taken care of?"

Eden went to the chest and removed Lucien's crystal from the Hopi artifact. She approached Lucien and draped his crystal around his neck.

"This crystal you wear is from the river of the water of life flowing from the throne of God and the lamb down from the great city of Moira. Made from the tears of the angels who fought alongside Michael against you. What some call Heaven. On each side of the river stands a tree of life, bearing crops of fruit. The twelve babies you rescued. The leaves of the trees are for healing, Lucien. Just as you have healed Samantha, but this healing is for all nations. No longer will you be cursed by what you did to our Father by saving Sam, Dusty, Gloria and the babies. You sacrificed your life," said Eden.

A montage of everything that Lucien did for others flashed before his eyes.

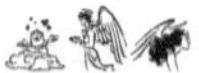

Lucien remembered times in his life at the Foster ranch when he healed a small dog that was hit by a car, a bird that could not fly to an elderly man who had a heart attack. Then he remembered Hidden Valley carrying Samantha. He laid her on the soft ground and placed his hands on her, starting her heart again. It was he when he burst into Oakridge Estates, who had saved Samantha from Banth. It was him, not Cassiel. It was him saving the Hybrids at Greenbrier. It was him rushing the children and women from Dulce. And the twelve babies. He has sacrificed so much for others. He remembered Sam's thoughts.

Am I dead? Is he an angel?

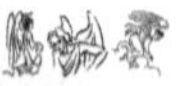

Eden took Lucien's hand. "Our Father will forgive you, Brother."

"*How?*"

"These words are true. The Lord, the God of the spirits of the prophets, sent his angels to prevent Banth and the underground dwellers they can't succeed. And they could have you or your son. This had to happen," Michael said.

"Why the charade?" He looked at his brothers and Eden. "Why did you lie to me all these years?" Tiny beads of sweat formed on his brow. A fury like no other boiled in the pit of his stomach. The lamps flickered as the bookshelves began to shake again.

"Lucien! Control yourself!" Jordan stood in front of him. "Your siblings did not lose faith and didn't give up on you, and neither did I."

"We were keeping you safe. Banth wanted you. Brother, we loved you. We still love you. We couldn't let Banth and the other 'Watchers' claim you again. You were His favorite. We were saving you from yourself. Can't you see that Brother?" said Michael.

They gathered around Lucien. A bright light shone all around them.

"You cannot give life or raise the dead, but that's what you've done. Before you were reincarnated, you could not read minds; only the Holy Trinity can. The Fallen can't be in more than one place at a time or alter time and you can!" Gabe said.

"Lucien, you've changed. You can heal, and that alone is a gift from our Father His favorite. He gave you that gift to see what you would do with that power. You are not the same as you were from the beginning. You are how you were supposed to be. You stepped in to save Samantha and the others. When your DNA would have never, you saved Dusty and the hybrids, and the women and children at Dulce," Nathan said.

"It goes against everything he stood for," Gabe said, putting his hand on Lucien's shoulder.

Lucien turned away as if to leave.

"Brother, look at me. Hell's mandate is to appear to humans as good and do so in every way possible—to the point of raising religions against religions and good things and then turn on them. Things that humans will follow and believe is the light, and it's the dark."

Michael continued. "What Hell cannot do is sacrifice for love above themselves. You were being kept from the light before. Now your sacrifices will be rejected by Hell. Do you understand? Gloria was forced to use her body as a vessel to bring forth the Morning Star—you that was cast into the dirt. You already had goodness in you. From the first moment, our Father created you before you were reincarnated until now."

"We have been protecting you from yourself. Don't you see?" Eden said.

"Lucien, you are not evil, and you are not alien. You are from the light and so is your son. The darkness cannot sacrifice themselves for the light, and that is what you have done. And once our Father sees this, he will accept you into Moira. God has forgiven your generational sins for your sacrifices. You were going to sacrifice yourself for Samantha," Michael said.

"The other dimension is real you saw it, and the veil is open, and you and Sam and the baby can be saved, just like your soul." Michael put both hands on Lucien's shoulders again. "Humans created ETs because they feared the Watchers the most."

"What are you saying? Aliens and UFOs are from..."

"Yes, humans think they are seeing aliens when in fact they are seeing angels and demons all along," Jordan interrupted.

"The Illuminati thought if humans knew the truth that angels and demons have been walking the earth since the beginning of time, it would have caused hysteria," Michael said.

"Yes, Lucien, even are great artists knew it too."

His gaze went to the paintings on the wall.

"How will I know if our Father forgives me?" Lucien looked at his sister.

"When the matrix and the veil is lifted, and you can leave Earth."

"What if it doesn't open? And Sam?"

"She will perish," Jordan said.

"What about Ory?" said Samantha, standing in the doorframe of the vault, cradling Ory.

"Sam?" Lucien said. His gaze went to Jordan, who looked shocked as well.

She settled near Lucien and took his hand and held Ory tight to her breast.

"Did you really think I couldn't hear? Your voices echo throughout the compound."

"Do you hear what they are saying I am?"

"I heard every word." She looked Lucien in the eye.

"Do you believe what they are saying is true?"

"If any word is true, they have lied to you all this time."

"She's right. How do I know you are telling me the truth now?" A rush of cold air filled the room.

"Will you love him any less?" Eden whispered.

"You are saying my son is...I can't even say the words."

"Yes."

"Lucien, you came from His light. Does it matter where the light came from? I accepted you all along. Whether the blood that runs through my veins is alien, or otherworldly being's, it's your blood. Will you love this baby any less?" Sam asked.

Lucien didn't answer as he gazed at Ory. "He matters."

"Who cares where you are from?"

"What if that portal doesn't open?"

"Then it's our time," Sam said.

"There is no Moira..."

"Lucien, Moira is real. It's just not what you thought it was," Daniel said. "Isn't that right, Brother? Sister?"

"What about my son?"

"Lucien, how can you doubt he isn't your son?" Sam said.

"Is he my son?" Lucien's gaze met Jordan's."

"Yes, he is yours," Gabe said.

"What about Sam? Is she here because of my healing? Or some darker force?"

"Lucien—"

Sam looked down at the ground and brought Ory close to her.

"Your healing is from the light. You must believe that Lucien," Jordan said, settling next to Sam.

"Why do I wear the medallion?" He ripped his medallion off with the inscription Cor. 15:40. "Corinthians 15:40 ... Is this a lie?"

"There are also heavenly bodies, and there are earthly bodies, but the splendor of the heavenly bodies is one kind, and the splendor of the earthly bodies is another. It was probably a warning," said Eden.

"Zoris said Sam is special. Her blood mixed. She did not die. Nephilim's offspring never conceive a child with such splendid blood. That's what he said. "Apparently, they were wrong. Sam is dying she's rejecting my blood?"

"Maybe they're wrong, and it can still be a virus from Dulce," Sam said.

"No."

"Earth is not a haven for the three of you now. Even though our Father forgives you. With or without you there's Banth and the other 'Watchers' who want to destroy the light and take over this Earth," Cassiel said.

"It's a war between good and evil on earth," Nathan added. "They brought the war in heaven down to earth."

"The virus will destroy the humans and Earth will die, and a new Earth will arise if that's its fate," Gabe said.

"If we leave and Lucien is forgiven will it prevent earth's destruction?"

"We won't know until then."

How will we know?" asked Samantha.

"If the portal does not open?" Jordan said.

"Then it's fate."

"All this time." Lucien looked at the ground. He thought about Sam and the baby.

"Brother, your blood is not mixing anymore with Sam we know that. She and the baby are going to die unless they leave. The serum is just a quick fix. You must go to London like we planned. It is the only way."

"Like I don't know that!" He picked up the chair and threw it. Sam backed away, crouching.

"Lucien!"

"Why were you going make me go through having surgery? Was it a test?"

"No. We were hoping your father would have mercy," Jordan said.

"Maybe a test on His part. Maybe. To see if you would sacrifice your life for Sam."

Eden went to Lucien's side. "What's happening was supposed to happen to you." She looked at each one of them.

"Ory will live, I know he will; all of you will. The portal is your only hope. You must leave." Lucien looked at his sister. "For now."

"Once both you and the baby leave through the portal and are given the antidote, you may come back someday," Michael agreed.

"What's the antidote?"

"His forgiveness."

"Why doesn't our Father just come down here and heal her if he is all powerful?"

"No one ever sees him. His greatness is too powerful; he is all but light. It doesn't work like that."

32 FORGIVENESS

Dusk was beginning to fall on Foster Ranch. Lucien closed his fists and went outside and watched the sunset. Eden was right behind him.

He climbed the satellite's ladder and pushed a button, retracting the lenses.

"If we are not from there, why even bother?"

"But we are, Lucien."

"From the sky?"

"Believe what you want, Morning Star," she said.

"Morning Star," Lucien remembered. "He called me his Morning Star."

"Because your light was the brightest of all his angels like the Morning Star," Eden said. "You are beginning to remember."

"What if the portal doesn't work? What if it really is a virus that Banth made that is killing Sam? And no matter how much forgiveness he gives us it doesn't work."

"All the bloodwork in the world and ultrasounds and body scans can't deny what our Father already knows."

"This is so surreal."

"I know it's a lot to take all at once, but in time you will and understand why we did what we did."

"If I have any time left you mean. What I don't understand is Cassiel switched places with me. But when?"

"From the moment Ory was born."

"We had to get you out of there, you were more important than the baby at that point. We didn't know exactly how you both got back. Someone in the alliance maybe. They knew who you were."

"They kept us separate at first. I never saw their faces. Just shadows. Their faces were hidden."

"Did you ever wonder what was happening to you?"

"Why didn't they figure out Cassiel wasn't me?"

"Angels can take many forms."

"So much deception."

"For the good of mankind."

"I don't even know how I left or got to Greenbrier? I believed they were Moiran's and the Black Knight was our mother ship."

She just nodded."

"I just thought that it all had to do with the alliance. I believed it had to do with the death of the FBI agent. I assume that's all a lie."

"No, there is an alliance with your government. The Illuminati are the only ones who know the truth. They did make a pact with who they thought were are extra-terrestrials from another world just not the world they thought. And they were given technology to keep quiet."

"Who else knows that aliens and UFO'S are not what they thought they were?'

"Pope John Paul II knew."

"Three Secrets of Fátima"

"Yes. One of the secrets.

"They weren't going to let you go. Banth and the No Whites were searching for you. They were more concerned with Sam when they abducted her and took her in the old cellar at Oak Ridge Estates. Dr. O'Neil was working behind his back. She was more concerned with baby Ory at the time. Do you understand now? They took the baby. Banth must have found out," Eden said.

"Isn't there some sort of rule in Hell once you fall you're out for good?" Lucien said.

"The Black Knight is not hell but a vessel. Dulce is the pit. A stopping ground."

"Hell, on Earth."

"Correct."

There are a secret portals like the wormholes. If they really want to find a way in, they can."

"And steal Ory. And take him back to Dulce."

"They didn't steal him. We sacrificed him."

"To the pit. Why? He was just a baby."

"Your son was supposed to die and not survive."

"The blood marrow transplant."

"But he did."

33 GOOD-BYE

We gathered one last time in the Fosters' conference room. Members of Division Six who also knew the truth, Nathan Moore AKA Rafael, Zoris, and Landson Shaw all angels working together to make our departure happen. The underground corridor never had so many visitors at one time.

"It has to work; otherwise, the fate of the Earth is on the line," Shaw said.

"If anything, it's the first time ever in history that humans and EBE are working together." Jordan stood, gazing at the map.

"You mean angels and demons, don't you?" Lucien said.

No one seemed to think Lucien's coy remark was amusing.

"If our calculations are correct, the timing is perfect. For the first time in ninety-nine years, a total solar eclipse will occur across the globe," Nathan Moore said, pulling up a map of the world on a virtual screen.

"The eclipse will happen coast to coast from

Oregon to South Carolina spanning fourteen states and across Europe. The darkest phase will happen in London at Stonehenge's portal, which, over a span of almost two hours, everyone will experience more than two minutes of total darkness. Then it will happen again in twenty-four hours from New York to Oregon, forming a complete X across the United States. This has never happened in the history of Earth," Jordan said.

"The energy it will produce will open the portal. It will open." Nathan gaze met Jordan's. "The eclipse will amplify the signal to get you to the portal to the other plane," Michael said.

Jordan took a vial from the small refrigerator in his lab.

"Samantha, dear, this will get you to where you and the baby need to go," Jordan said.

"Tell me...why do I feel this is not real?"

"It's real, my dear, and you are a big part of mankind's history."

Jordan lifted my shirt sleeve and smiled while he gave me a bit more of serum to get me to London.

He did the same thing to baby Ory. A wail came from his tiny lungs.

I quickly picked him up and gently kissed his cheek.

"Everything is set in motion," Michael said, joining us.

"I got a chopper to get you to Crystal Beach in

Texas. As you requested, Sam," Michael said.

"The beach?" Lucien turned to me.

"I want to walk the beach one last time on Earth before we leave for London."

Lucien raised an eyebrow.

"I want to see the ocean one last time, what's wrong with that?"

"Moira has more beaches than you can count," Jordan said.

"But it's not Earth."

"No, it's not," Eden said, taking Ory from my arms. "It's more beautiful than any beach on Earth, and the sand is like stepping on velvet, the colors are more vibrant, and the air, oh the air is sweet as chocolate." She danced around the room with Ory. "The grass is greener than any lawn here on Earth, and ohhh, the music...a choir of angels singing." She laughed.

She gave me back Ory.

"Was it all an act?" I asked.

"I don't follow."

"Your obvious dislike for me," I said.

"I couldn't let you think I was an angel, now could I?" She smiled.

"Hmmm."

"I'll let you ponder that for a while."

Jordan and Dejaha Zoris along with all the Fosters left the foyer of the Fosters' Ranch on the upper level. They watched a black Navigator pull up the driveway on the security cameras.

"I guess this is it," I said with a nervous clearing of my throat. "My father doesn't know who you truly are? Right?"

"He thinks I'm EBE an extraterrestrial biological entity that I am."

"I guess you're right." He picked up Ory and took my hand. I started to choke up.

"Wait."

"Take all the time you need." He brought Ory close to his chest and bent down and kissed his forehead.

"I don't know if I can do this." I caught his gaze.

"Yes, you can. You are stronger now than you ever were. The girl afraid of heights, who was afraid to drive, went up against the worst possible enemy. You conquered your deepest, darkest fears. You tackled the worst possible enemies and won. And now, this next challenge is the most important. You saved me from a fate of total darkness."

"How can you say I saved you? You saved me."

"We saved each other."

"It's time. You better go before your dad tries to stop you." Eden smiled, taking Ory from Lucien.

We met my father and Kate outside near the Camaro. Saying goodbye to my father forever was a lot easier than I thought. I would see him again hopefully.

I looked at him carefully one last time. His hair

had grown gray, and his eyes were tired. I never got to know the woman beside him.

At least he would not be alone. Kate stood in the background, giving us a private moment to ourselves. "I never thought I would have to say goodbye to you this way," my father said, hugging me.

"The alternative is much worse, you know that," I said, choking back tears.

"There is no other way? Are you sure?"

"For now, this the only way, Daddy. Don't make it harder than it has to be." My dad held me tight. I didn't want to let him go.

Eden brought Ory over, handing him to my father. He held Ory close and kissed his forehead. The others kept their distance while we said our last goodbyes.

"As long as you're okay, that's all that matters."

"You have Kate. That's wonderful, Dad."

"What about the virus?"

"Jordan said the virus is under control. They have a vaccine, which is good. But there will be many more. You have to make sure you stay away from big crowds. There will be times I can communicate with you, but there will be other times I can't, so take care of yourself," I said, trying to calm him.

"If that's what Jordan said."

I watched my dad with the baby. His only grandchild. My heart ached for him. I tried to fight the tears from falling. But they made their way down my cheeks, burning all the way. I wished there was a way for the serum to last more than a few hours.

For a moment Finn was beside us. He just watched not saying anything.

"Maybe there will be a cure, and you can come back." I didn't have the heart to tell him I could never come back.

"It could happen." I wiped my eyes.

My dad started to cry. He hugged the baby tight. "I'll never get to play ball with you." Tears flooded my eyes, making it hard to see. My dad handed Ory back to me.

"Will I ever see you again?" my father asked.

"I don't know. Maybe." I could see Lucien approaching from the ranch.

Kate joined us. "I'm sorry I didn't get to know you, Sam," Kate said, taking my hand.

"You take care of him, okay?" I said while Lucien took Ory from my dad's arms.

I hugged my dad and Kate and then Dad again. My dad's feet were slow as he made his way to the car.

He opened the car door and looked back at me. I smiled, wiping a tear. They got in the Navigator.

I settled near Lucien while they drove away. Jordan slowly made his way to our side.

"Sam, it's getting late. You don't have much time before the serum runs out," Jordan said.

"I know... I know." I hugged Ory and rested my

chin on his sweet-smiling head.

34 MORNING STAR

Jordan embraced Lucien once last time. Daniel and Cassiel, Gabe and Michael all hugged. The sky opened with a ray of sunshine beaming down on Lucien. His skin changed to a golden brown, and his snowy diamond eyes blazed with white light. He stood among his angel brothers, but their beauty did not come even close to the Morning Star. When the sun's rays touched Ory, his skin radiated ivory instead of his father's sun-kissed skin. Lucien felt it was sign from above. Good or bad, he was at peace with what was to come.

Eden started to go back inside. "Hey?"

Lucien went after her.

"You're going to let me leave without a goodbye?"

"I don't like goodbyes. I don't want to get all mushy on you. It's a sign of weakness."

"You've never been weak once in your entire life."

"I'm a good actress."

"You can come with us."

"And leave our uncle?" She didn't smile.

"Don't you angels have more important things to do now that you don't have to babysit me anymore?"

"Oh, Lucien you have no idea. Our work here has just begun now that the pit is opened. Not only will Banth want to intercede again, but there are also the other Fallen that must go back to the pit. In your other life, you unleashed two hundred million fallen angels on Earth."

"I'm sorry, I don't remember any of that."

"I know you don't." She smiled. "And it's a good thing you don't. They are well organized now. There's no telling what they are capable of. There are the hybrids and ranked by class based on power. Now, without hope of regaining their prince, someone will take leadership."

"Won't Banth just assume the position?"

"You'd think so. But like your president, the Illuminati may decide otherwise. The ones at Greenbrier surrendered to the light. But, Lucien, there is an invisible war going on."

"It would be so much easier for you and the others if I could stay."

"You have work to do in Moira. You were forgiven, hopefully, but we won't know for sure until you are inches from the portal."

"You don't sound convincing, Eden."

"I don't mean to sound like a pessimist. I know in my heart our Father will forgive you and Samantha will be saved. We have to have faith."

"You sure you can't come with us? I would like you on my side there. Ory will need to be cared for. What if the antidote doesn't work on her?"

"I don't think Zoris would go to all the trouble with the alliance if he had doubts. I can't go. None of us can. We are needed here. Or until it's time for our Father's return to this plane."

"Hmmm. Is it true the virus is under control?"

"I think Jordan just told Sam that not to worry her."

"Do you think the virus will destroy Earth?"

"It may. The Division says they have it contained, but viruses have a way of finding a way to survive. Especially if you aren't forgiven."

"I can visit in time."

"You can if you stay in the light and away from the contra dark."

"You don't think it's possible for me, do you?"

"I think of everything you've done for Sam and the people in Dulce. I believe the odds are stacked for you, not against you."

"The odds... I fought the desire to not help those humans at Dulce. But not Sam. I knew I had to help her."

"Too bad Sam knows your secret. I don't think she really understands what you truly are. It hasn't sunk in yet."

"Will she accept me truly?"

"She has no choice now, does she?"

He forced a smile. He hoped he hadn't made a mistake by finding Jordan's secret vault. Maybe he could have gone on living the life he knew.

"We should have told you all along."

"I don't know, I may have been too young to understand. How can she?"

"Maybe some things were better left unsaid."

Lucien pulled her into his arms. Tears streamed down Eden's face. "Do you forgive us?"

"Can I answer that once I know the portal will open?"

"He will accept you."

"How? When I don't accept who I am, or what I am."

"You will."

"One last thing."

"What is it?"

"If I was named the Morning Star, why does my skin change color in the sun?"

"You skin is made up of iridium and sulfur. It was your punishment. A constant reminder to the lake of fire and brimstone. The scars near your tattoos you always had. It's a seal from where your wings were clipped. It pains me to be the one to tell you."

"I truly fell from heaven." A shadow appeared on his face. A glimpse of what he truly once was.

"You are no longer him. You were reborn."

A second of silence passed.

"Let's go!" Nathan broke their farewell.

Sam came running back with Ruby.

"Oh my God, we can't forget Ruby girl!"

Ruby barked, and her ruby-red eyes shone.

"Is she allowed?"

"Ruby's a Cherubim yes of course she is," said Nathan.

Samantha and Lucien walked to the chopper with Ruby by their side. He turned one last time to look at the home he only knew.

Lucien helped Samantha board the chopper. Once inside, he and Samantha kept their eyes on the ground below.

Jordan and his siblings watched, their hair blowing in the wind. The chopper's blades took them high.

They both looked out the window until the images below faded.

Neither of them spoke on the ride to the airport. Ruby sat between them. Sam petted Ruby while Lucien pondered the next chapter of their life. The trip didn't take long to Crystal Beach. Landson Shaw's pilot made sure they didn't waste too much time. The flight was under two hours.

The chopper landed at Crystal Beach airport, Samantha and Lucien's last destination before they flew to Stonehenge in Wiltshire, England.

35 HELLO ANGEL

Dear Emma,

The sky is painted in blue across the horizon with not a cloud in sight. I watch the seagulls fly by, relishing their sound while Lucien strolls the beach holding our child.

I am mesmerized gazing at the waves crashing the shore. The foamy blue water washes my sadness away.

I wanted to see the ocean one last time before I leave my home.

Lucien says there are beaches where we are going. However, none will be my home sweet home.

I sought to hold on to this view and cherish it forever in my heart. The silver-edged clouds splashing against the blue of the heavens is what I will remember. I am not sure if I am going to Moira or heaven.

Moments ago, I walked along the shore, following Lucien's footprints in the sand. I savored the feel of the wet sand between my toes. I took in a breath of the sea-salt air and gazed down at the seaweed that washed in with the tide—one more minute that's all I wanted. I wished I could alter time like Lucien.

I stepped over a crab making its way to the pier and smiled. The sun's rays beamed all around us. This moment right now is my heaven on Earth.

Jordan said Earth, Moira, and Heaven are the same. They are so close that there's only a veil separating them. I am not so sure what I believe. I may never be sure.

There you have it Emma the truth... It's a good thing I didn't tell you all those years ago about Lucien's identity because at the time it would have been a lie. Does it change how I feel about him? No.

Was it all in my head? Maybe. Was it merely a dream? I will let you decide.

Love always,

Sam

Years later

I put my journal in an envelope and sealed it. I took off a gold chain with a key from around my neck. The key was to a safe-deposit box on Earth. I'd been wearing it for over forty Earth years and had never taken it off until now.

I took in a deep breath and looked up at the cloudless sky of Moira which looks and feels like another planet of its own but in another dimension. The Fosters still call it Moria. No words could describe its beauty. The colors were brighter and more vivid than any on Earth. The foamy ocean water glistened at the shore. The sand looked like the sand on any beach, but it felt like velvet, just like Eden said it would. I walked over to Lucien and handed him the envelope. I pushed the wind-blown hair out of my eyes.

"You sure about this?" Lucien said, dusting his hands of sand. He took the envelope.

"Yes. It's time. Eden can do it for me," I said, handing him the key. "This will open my father's safe deposit box on earth. I gave her strict instructions what to do with it."

In the distance, I could see my son. His coal-black hair was tousled from the wind. He smiled at me. His eyes radiated the same snowy diamonds as his father. I smiled, watching him walk hand in hand with two small children, a boy, and a girl. Their hair was the color of wheat. Behind them was his beautiful wife. Just like Ory, her cool blonde hair was wind-blown from the ocean breeze. I watched her stop to pick up sea shells and put them in a sand bucket.

"He has turned into such a handsome man, our Ory. He is the image of his father."

"Ory!" Lucien bellowed with a chuckle.

He waved. Behind him were Michael, Gabriel,

Cassiel, Daniel, and Eden, still in their glory, smiling and laughing. They ran after the children. Michael picked up my granddaughter and twirled her in the air. I couldn't help but laugh. Lucien caught my gaze and took my hand as we caught up with them

"Our granddaughter is laughing so hard she can't catch her breath."

"Her laughter is like the taste of chocolate," I said.

Eden skipped after my grandson, kicking up sand. And right above them, a white dove glided above the clouds. I exhaled a sigh of peace. I quit asking Lucien and the others if were merely dead and what we're now are just spirits. A mere human can't comprehend what we indeed are now. I've come to accept I am an EBE and leave it at that.

Many years later.

Pittsburgh, Pennsylvania

"Would you look at that?" a young man said, getting out of a U-Haul. The evening sunset decorated the Western Pennsylvania sky, kissing it with mauve and violet crests.

"Breathtaking. Hello, angel," the young woman said.

"Who are you talking to?"

"The red cardinal perched on Gram's fence. Folklore says their messengers from heaven."

They stepped onto the porch and unlocked the front door. As soon as they did the cardinal flew away.

"Man, does it smell musky." He pulled back the drapes and opened a window.

They stood back and surveyed the home.

"Looks like we have our work cut out for us, huh?"

"Do you want to start now or wait until morning?"

"I say the sooner we start, the sooner we can leave."

"Hope there's coffee in one of those cabinets."

"Can you believe all this junk?"

"She never read her mail by the looks of all those unopened letters piled up on her desk."

"These have dates on them going way back."

They walked into the living room.

"I had no idea Grams was such a hoarder, did you?"

"Nope."

The young man opened and closed a box on the dining room table.

"Yep! She sure was a hoarder."

He knocked into a shelf, and a package fell.

"Ellie, look at this."

"It hasn't been opened."

"I wonder how long it's been here. There's no return address or postage. And look at this strange seal." He handed it to Ellie.

"I've never seen anything like it."

"Open it."

"Why do I get the feeling its best unopened."

"Just do it."

They sat down on the sofa.

"It's someone's journal."

"There's a letter."

"What does it say?"

Ellie took a breath and began to read.

"Dear Emma,

I'm writing this while watching my grandchildren make sandcastles. The sun and the salt of the ocean remind me of him. It reminded me of you, also. You're probably wondering why I'm contacting you after all these years. I ask myself the same question. I thought it was time you knew the truth, especially you, dear friend..."

THE END.

"All flesh is not the same flesh: but there is one kind of flesh of men, another flesh of beasts, another of fishes, and another of birds." Corinthians" 15:39

Acknowledgements:

Special thanks to Michael Seacy RIP Writer, Producer, Director at Seacy film Australia. He taught me evil can never sacrifice itself for love.

John Ventre Pennsylvania State Director. The UFOLOGIST: The Haunting of John Ventre. This forever changed my mind on UFOs and alien beings.

Sherry Hinkle author Artist/Writer at The Dulce Material, Dulce Papers, Dulce Sketches
The Holy Bible King James version

UFO: Uncovering the Truth
Learn more about J.E. Nicassio Author J. E. Nicassio
J.E.Nicassio@jennie3963
www.authorjenicassio.com